Communities of Musical Practice

Every day people come together to make music. Whether amateur or professional, young or old, jazz enthusiasts or rock stars, what is common to all of these musical groups is the potential to create communities of musical practice (CoMP). Such communities are created through practices: ways of engaging, rules, membership, roles, identities and learning that is both shared through collective musical endeavour and situated within certain sociocultural contexts. Ailbhe Kenny investigates CoMP as a rich model for community engagement, musical participation and transformation in music education.

This book is the first to produce a valid and reliable in-depth study of music communities using a community of practice (CoP) framework – in this case focusing on the social process of musical learning. Employing case study research within Ireland, three illustrations from particular sociocultural, genre-specific, economic and geographical contexts are examined: an adult amateur jazz ensemble, a youth choir and an online platform for Irish traditional music. Each case is analysed as a distinct community and phenomenon offering sharpened understandings of each sub-culture with specific findings presented for each community.

Ailbhe Kenny is Lecturer in Music Education at Mary Immaculate College, University of Limerick, Ireland. She is a Fulbright Scholar, holds a PhD from the University of Cambridge and publishes internationally in journals, handbooks and edited volumes on music, arts and teacher education.

SEMPRE Studies in The Psychology of Music
Series Editors:
Graham Welch, University of London, UK, Adam Ockelford, Roehampton University, UK and Ian Cross, University of Cambridge, UK

The theme for the series is the psychology of music, broadly defined. Topics include (i) musical development at different ages, (ii) exceptional musical development in the context of special educational needs, (iii) musical cognition and context, (iv) culture, mind and music, (v) micro to macro perspectives on the impact of music on the individual (from neurological studies through to social psychology), (vi) the development of advanced performance skills and (vii) affective perspectives on musical learning. The series presents the implications of research findings for a wide readership, including user-groups (music teachers, policy makers, parents) as well as the international academic and research communities. This expansive embrace, in terms of both subject matter and intended audience (drawing on basic and applied research from across the globe), is the distinguishing feature of the series, and it serves SEMPRE's distinctive mission, which is to promote and ensure coherent and symbiotic links between education, music and psychology research.

For a full list of titles in this series, please visit www.routledge.com

Other titles in the series include:

Artistic Practice as Research in Music: Theory, Criticism, Practice
Edited by Mine Doğantan-Dack

The Tangible in Music
Marko Aho

Creative Teaching for Creative Learning in Higher Music Education
Edited by Elizabeth Haddon and Pamela Burnard

Music, Technology and Education
Edited by Andrew King and Evangelos Himonides

Communities of Musical Practice

Ailbhe Kenny

Routledge
Taylor & Francis Group

LONDON AND NEW YORK

First published 2016
by Routledge
2 Park Square, Milton Park, Abingdon, Oxon OX14 4RN

and by Routledge
711 Third Avenue, New York, NY 10017

First issued in paperback 2017

Routledge is an imprint of the Taylor & Francis Group, an informa business

© 2016 Ailbhe Kenny

British Library Cataloguing in Publication Data
A catalogue record for this book is available from the British Library

Library of Congress Cataloging in Publication Data
Catalog record for this book has been requested

ISBN 13: 978-1-138-09245-7 (pbk)
ISBN 13: 978-1-4724-5675-5 (hbk)

Typeset in Times New Roman
by Swales & Willis Ltd, Exeter, Devon, UK

Contents

Figures

Tables

Foreword

Music is an interesting practice for social learning theorists. It is anchored in cultural traditions and yet invites interpretation, innovation and in many genres, improvisation. It is intensely social. It brings people together, whether to produce it or enjoy it. And it is intensely individual. Musical skills require hours of demanding practice and musical inspiration springs from very personal emotions. Even in group performances, each musician makes an individual contribution.

Music is also a particular identity. Because of my children I have had the opportunity to observe musicians in their communities. One thing struck me. Musicians seem to find a distinct pleasure in recognising each other. The music business is as competitive as any, and yet you can witness an overriding sense of mutual appreciation and companionship among musicians. I have seen oldtimers truly excited by the promise of a gifted newcomer – the discovery of one of them, the potential of better music. This recognition quickly translates into joint practice. Musicians love to join in or find someone who can join in. The identification is with the art and the social fabric it weaves.

So music lends itself to a social learning perspective: how communities form around musical practice, how one becomes a practitioner and takes on the identity of a musician, and how the practice evolves out of the dynamics of the community and its members. It is worth a good look – to better understand the making of music and musicians, and in the process to better understand the complex nature of human learning.

Etienne Wenger

Preface

Boys called Danny and gardens named Sally

As a young child, I sang with a group called the 'Little Gaelic Singers' in New York City. As the name of the group suggests, we were Irish (or Irish-American in some cases), little (helped by the fact we were children) and of course sang. The title of the choral group delineated our identity and instantly access to the group itself. This was, after all, no ordinary group of young singers. First, we acted as a 'backing choir' to the famous Irish tenor Frank Patterson. This meant a busy gigging schedule with highlights including the making of music videos in the Botanical Gardens to performances on Broadway. It also translated to an audition process, the type of audition process that required a personal connection to even get an audition. High standards were a must and behind the green ribbons, bright smiles and white dresses was a strict rehearsal schedule and marketing of an 'authentic' Irish brand.

I remember my mother walking my sister and me to rehearsals, my brother too young to join the choir but brought along, trailing behind. I recall her meeting up with other Irish mothers (the fathers rarely featured, as weekends meant time for 'nixers' in the building trade), eager to make friends and share news of 'home'. It was the 80s and we were mostly immigrants having made our way from an island that offered us little to a city of dreams. The group represented a common bond of 'Irishness' within a metropolis of millions. We sang songs of the villages, towns and cities we had left among tunes about boys called Danny and gardens named Sally. To us children, the lyrics could have been about ice cream and bicycles; to the adults they meant much more.

I was six years old but remember the rehearsals well. They took place in a school on Saturdays, and the differences in furniture, posters and books compared to my school fascinated me. Among these alien classrooms, we sang scales, exercises and songs for Frank Patterson's wife, Eily O'Grady. She banged out notes on the piano as we strained to reach the 'high notes'. I was put in the soprano line and my sister with the altos. A hierarchy of voice quality was assumed. This classification remained with us for life, with my older sister never believing she was as good a singer as me.

Eily was our maestro, with only occasional visits from 'the star' right before the performance. In fact, my main memory of Frank himself is of his back filling a black jacket and repeating the same line in every concert about 'loving America'. This became a running joke in our family for several years, recounted often during celebratory meals and toast-worthy occasions. Eily, like the other Irish mothers, was our guide, putting the hard work in and taking a place behind the piano in performance to allow her husband centre stage. She was not the only teacher, however. I learned from the older girls the notes to sing, where to stand and how to curl my hair for the stage. We spent hours playing, chatting and laughing in between long hours of rehearsal at various halls, venues and hotel rooms. I learned the routines, norms and behaviours required of performance where a smile on stage was valued as much as the sound that emerged. I experienced the thrill of applause, the glare of the spotlight and the excitement of looking into a sea of blackness where the audience sat.

The 'Little Gaelic Singers' required commitment not just from the boys and girls who sang but also from the broader support networks of families and friends to get us to rehearsal, travel to concerts, make packed lunches and clap the loudest. There were tensions as much as there were friendships. We were a community and I was a member. I belonged. Through writing this book I have come to realise that this was my first community of musical practice.

Acknowledgements

In the spirit of this book investigating communities of musical practice, the research and writing itself was the result of multiple and overlapping communities of practice.

I would like to acknowledge the hard work of the series editors as well as Laura Macy, Emma Gallon and Michael Bourne. This work owes a debt to Prof Pam Burnard at the University of Cambridge whose generosity of time, expertise and support is inimitable. I am also grateful to Fulbright as the book was completed as part of a Scholar Award at Teachers College, Columbia University and New York University. Support within my workplace, Mary Immaculate College, was of course also essential to the completion of this book. For these supports I would like to thank, first, my colleagues and head of department, Dr Micheal Finneran within the Department of Arts Education and Physical Education as well as the Research Office and Department of Music.

Many conversations occurred throughout the process of writing this book. I would like to particularly thank Prof Stephanie Pitts, Prof Karen Littleton, Dr Patricia Flynn, John Finney, Dr Etienne Wenger, Prof Jim Deegan, Dr Randall Allsup, Dr Alex Ruthmann, Dr Helen Phelan, Prof Mícheál Ó Súilleabháin, Dr Rosie Perkins and Dr Joanne Dillabough for providing insightful feedback along the way.

The support given me from close friends and siblings, Clíona and Emmet, was unwavering. My brother in particular gave most willingly of his design skills and talent which is deeply appreciated. To my mother, Eithne, my first and constant teacher – thank you. Finally, to my husband Richard, you know this work almost as intimately as I do and so with you I share the finishing line.

To the participants within this research, for letting me into your 'musical worlds', I am truly grateful. You are this research.

Abbreviations

CoP	Community of practice
CoMP	Community of musical practice
EU	European Union
AC	Arts Council (of Ireland)
MEP	Music Education Partnership
DES	Department of Education and Skills (Ireland)
DAHG	Department of the Arts, Heritage and the Gaeltacht (Ireland)
LJW	Limerick Jazz Workshop
CLYC	County Limerick Youth Choir
OAIM	Online Academy of Irish Music

Introduction

Every day people come together to make music. Whether amateur or professional, young or old, jazz enthusiasts or rock stars, what is common to all of these musical groups is the potential to create 'communities of musical practice' (CoMPs). Such communities are created through practices; rules, membership, roles, identities and learning that are both 'shared' through collective musical endeavour and 'situated' within certain sociocultural contexts. This book investigates CoMPs as a rich model for musical participation, community engagement and potential transformation in music education. Situated within a growing global concern for participation and creativity within local communities, the focus of the book is on how CoMPs are created and sustained through collaborative practices.

The primary concern of this book then is its examination of the social process of musical learning. The CoMP framework employed is theoretically based on a sociocultural learning model that is participatory, collaborative, takes account of context and value systems and is seen as a 'life-long' journey of musical participation. Identity formation within communities is also crucial to this view of learning where identities are viewed as negotiated in practice. The book operationalises a CoMP model for the selection, analysis and interpretation of the research undertaken. Framed within this sociocultural theory of learning, the book conceptually, methodologically, theoretically and experientially seeks to cross into 'new terrain' to capture the complexities that lie within musical communities.

The 'community of practice' (CoP) model (Lave & Wenger, 1991; Wenger, 1998) has gained significant traction in contemporary discourse and so there has been a growing interest in its application among numerous disciplines including music education and community music. This book builds on and expands the use of the CoP framework within music research to contribute to theory building and deepen our understandings of musical communities. A sustained discussion on group music-making through a CoP lens is offered to penetrate thinking about collective music-making within local contexts.

The central research question for this study is: how are 'communities of musical practice' developed and sustained in practice? Nestled within this overarching research question, the book seeks to examine the actual musical and community 'practices' as they occurred within potential CoMPs. There is a particular focus on issues relating to behaviours, roles and identities as they manifest through musical and social interactions. The interplay between the 'local' practices and the broader structures and issues surrounding CoMPs also has significant relevance to this consideration. A series of sub-questions to guide the study thus emerge:

- What actual practices of music teaching, learning and participation occur within CoMPs?
- What is the relationship between community, music and learning within CoMPs?
- What are the actions, roles, behaviours, experiences and relationships within CoMPs?
- How are musical identities formed and informed within CoMPs?

These questions allow for a focused discussion rooted in micro-musical practices that address macro themes of musical participation, learning, identity and belonging.

Why this book?

There are both personal and academic reasons for writing this book. Personally, I have always been involved in local arts activities such as choirs, drama groups, ensembles and musical societies since childhood (see Preface). From purely a musical standpoint, I have been immersed in music both in an amateur and professional manner throughout my life and took private music tuition in voice, piano and guitar during childhood and into adulthood. This rich engagement in music merged into an academic interest when I studied music alongside education at university.

In my career as a primary teacher and music education specialist I directed school choirs, musicals and cross-disciplinary arts performances, thus engaging with the wider school community in this way. I also worked in a children's cultural centre which gave further insight into the inner workings of arts organisations. Since entering academia I continue to make links between school and community music in varying capacities, through multiple projects. Stemming from these experiences, I maintain a keen interest in observing and questioning what makes musical communities 'tick'; how they learn and form ways of being with each other. This I have always believed involves an intersection of practices that are at once both musical and social.

The book aims to build upon knowledge about how musical communities make, learn and share music. The research presented also acts as a point of departure from previous studies in offering fresh perspectives to examine how, why and where musical learning takes place within communities. Close-up illustrations from practice illuminate what is actually happening on the ground within musical communities through participant and observer perspectives. Sociocultural theoretical frameworks and in particular the CoP model form a key role in informing and shaping these insights. Particular emphasis is given to the importance of making music as a collaborative, 'situated' endeavour for informing teaching and learning approaches within community, school and varying institutional levels.

The context and study

Employing case study research within the Republic of Ireland (hereafter Ireland), three illustrations from particular sociocultural, genre-specific, economic and geographical contexts are examined; an adult amateur jazz ensemble, a youth choir and an online Irish traditional music web platform. Each case is analysed as a distinct community and phenomenon offering sharpened understandings of each sub-culture with specific findings presented for each community. These evidence-based insights are situated within broader macro music education practices, both on and offline, where comparative conclusions are drawn. Thus, the book aims to illuminate the relationship between community, music and learning through its discussion of collaborative music-making practices.

Qualitative data on the three cases was gathered over a nine-month period (October 2010–June 2011). Investigating the community and musical practices of the three CoMPs endeavoured to ground the research in the 'real world' (Robson, 2002). The discussion of findings frame or 'map out' the 'musical worlds' (Finnegan, 2007) of each case. The three illustrations are discussed within broad community and musical practice themes but also take into account practices that were particularly distinctive within each case. Context is central to this examination. Each of the cases examined represented a *potential* CoMP that was situated in the mid-west of Ireland and was government-supported to some degree. The online case reflects the contemporary fast-growing online 'place' for musical communities to inhabit. Due to the sociocultural theories taken up in this book to examine CoMPs, a brief overview of the Irish music education landscape, followed by a description of each community to be discussed, are outlined here.

The Irish music education landscape

There is presently a multi-faceted provision of music education in Ireland. A general music education is largely delivered through a music curriculum in schools and instrumental/performance music education is typically provided through private or voluntary means. Music education within further and higher education offered across 12 institutions has expanded the diversity of courses offered in recent years including degrees and courses in jazz music, Irish traditional music, popular music and music technology. Music education in Ireland has a long history of debate. Contentious issues focus on formal contexts where inequalities of access, quality assurance, funding and resource scarcities, lack of joined-up thinking and shared vision, as well as specialist versus generalist teacher debates abound (Arts Council of Ireland, 2008a; Heneghan, 2001; Herron, 1985; Kenny, 2011; McCarthy, 1999; Moore, 2014; Music Network, 1997, 2003).

Tensions exist not just for music education but all arts education provision in Ireland. The national 'Points of Alignment' (2008) report highlights the existing dichotomy between two separate departments for the arts and education (Arts Council Ireland, 2008a, p. 45): 'One of the great deficiencies has been the lack of a coherent vision or cohesive national plan. Among other things, this has led to much fragmentation, and lack of co-ordination'. As well as such continued fragmentation, cuts to arts funding within recent years have caused further pressure on music education in Ireland. In response to such pressures, the 'Arts in Education Charter' (Department of Education and Skills & Department of Arts Heritage and the Gaeltacht, 2013) aims to promote and develop arts education and arts in education among children, young people and third-level students through an integrated and collaborative approach across government departments, education agencies and arts organisations.

Music education outside of schools and universities in 'informal' or 'non-formal' settings has received much less attention in the country. These forms of music-making are widespread, however, through such activities as ensembles, bands, choirs, online platforms and peer groups. Some of this activity is led through arts organisations who have marked themselves out as key stakeholders in music education in Ireland. One such example is Comhaltas Ceoltóirí Éireann[1], who work to preserve and promote Irish traditional music both nationally and internationally mainly through organising classes and music sessions through hundreds of local branches. Taking the choral sector as another example, an Arts Council report revealed the existence of 400 choirs around the country with participation from 'a wide range of practitioners, including school, youth, church and cathedral choirs, choral societies and institution-based choirs' (Arts Council of Ireland, 2008b, p. 21). Since the inception of local government arts offices throughout the country, they too have taken a lead in music education where most of their work in music takes an education focus through activities such as musician residencies, workshops, grants and tuition (Kenny, 2009, 2011).

The music resource agency Music Network also provides countrywide access to high-quality music experiences to all ages through provision of concerts countrywide, development of musicians through activities such as performance opportunities and training courses, and advocacy work, as well as acting as an information resource. Their report 'A National System of Local Music Education Services – Report of a Feasibility Study' (Music Network, 2003) identified a gap in instrumental and vocal music education in Ireland and recommended the creation of publicly funded local Music Education Partnerships (MEPs) to address this. Eventually, in 2009, a national rollout was supported by philanthropic funding through the popular band U2 and the Ireland Funds. Governmental support followed and now a national music education programme entitled 'Music Generation'[2] aims to help children and young people (up to 18 years) access music education in local communities. The programme offers funding and support to local MEPs throughout Ireland on a competitive basis (see Flynn, 2012; Molloy & Flynn, 2013).

Due to Ireland's incremental development of the arts at both national and local levels (Kenny, 2009, 2011), an information gap exists on the practices within music and broader arts communities. This is particularly true for research outside

1 http://comhaltas.ie.
2 See www.musicgeneration.ie.

of formal educational institutions. Insights from the three illustrations provided in this book address the need for more research-informed developments in this area on a national level, all the while taking cognisance of macro-music education and community practices. The contextual particularities of each illustration are provided below.

Illustration 1: The Limerick Jazz Workshop

The Limerick Jazz Workshop (LJW) is an adult ensemble-based teaching and performing initiative based in Limerick city, in the mid-west region of Ireland.[3] Limerick city, it is claimed, 'has benefited from significant public and private sector investment over the past two decades' (McCafferty & O'Keeffe, 2009, p. 10). This stemmed from a national economic boom during that time within Ireland.[4] From an arts and cultural vantage, the investment during the boom in physical arts infrastructure is obvious through venues such as: the University of Limerick Concert Hall, Irish World Academy of Music and Dance, Lime Tree Theatre and Limerick City Gallery of Art. In addition, a national designation of 'city of culture' for 2014[5] saw increased development, focus and funding in the arts throughout the city.

The music 'scene' in Limerick city involves a plethora of music groups, ensembles or 'communities', some of which are supported by national and/or local government. The city boasts a wide spectrum of different forms of musical participation within different genres, ranging from the historically embedded brass and reed bands, to internationally acclaimed contemporary rock bands. 'Limerick Jazz' (www.limerickjazz.com)[6] represents the jazz genre of Limerick city and comprises the Limerick Jazz Society and the LJW. The two organisations are seen to complement one another under the brand 'Limerick Jazz', with the Jazz Society programming professional live jazz gigs in the city and a yearly jazz festival, while the LJW provides jazz ensemble teaching and performing environments.

The LJW was set up in 2007 as a not-for-profit body by members of the Limerick Jazz Society. It aims to provide 'community jazz education' (LJW website, 2015) by providing jazz ensemble teaching and performing opportunities with local expert tutors. At the time of writing, there are over 30 adult participants representing 14 nationalities within the LJW. The workshop has four instrumental ensembles which range from 'beginners' to 'advanced' status and for the purpose

---

3 Limerick city, within County Limerick, is the third largest city in Ireland (see Figure 2.1 for a map of Ireland). The city alone has a population of approximately 60,000 people as recorded in the 2011 census (see www.cso.ie).

4 The 'Celtic Tiger' was the term used to describe the economic boom Ireland experienced between 1995 and 2007. This rapid economic growth went into a dramatic reversal from 2008 onwards, resulting in a recession.

5 See limerickcityofculture.ie.

6 Aside from the main website, Limerick Jazz also has an internet presence on Myspace (http://www.myspace.com/limerickjazzworkshop) and Facebook (http://www.facebook.com/pages/Limerick-Jazz).

of rehearsal only, an extra vocalist ensemble. The LJW is government-supported through a grant from the Limerick City and County Council Arts Service,[7] rehearsal space through the Learning Hub,[8] and the provision of live jazz gigs through the Arts Council-funded Limerick Jazz Society. Modest private tuition fees are also paid by the participants to cover teaching costs.

Illustration 2: The County Limerick Youth Choir

The County Limerick Youth Choir (CLYC) is a choir for young people aged between 16 and 26 years of age in the mid-west of Ireland. The CLYC is based in County Limerick.[9] Regarding arts and cultural provision, the city of Limerick provides the surrounding county with many resources and various music 'scenes' of Limerick city. In addition, however, several other musical 'worlds' exist within Co. Limerick outside of the city. The county is especially rich in private music tuition with many music schools across multi-genres as well as Comhaltas branches. Choral music, community music singing groups and a music festival make up the music initiatives supported by government. The CLYC is fully supported by the Limerick Arts Office[10] through the provision of rehearsal space, payment of choral director fees, administrative support and subsidised choral trips.

The CLYC was established in September 2006 by the County Limerick Arts Office (Limerick City and County Local Authorities amalgamated in 2014). Singing classical and contemporary choral music, the youth choir comprises approximately 28 young people. The CLYC have a heavy performance schedule locally, nationally and internationally at a range of events, concerts and festivals. By the end of the fieldwork period, the choir were recipients of many awards and titles including: first prize at Limerick Sacred Music Festival (2008); National Youth Choir of the Year (Navan Choral Festival, 2010); Best Youth Choir (Limerick Festival of Church Music, 2010); and first prize in the National Competition for Church Music (Cork International Choral Festival, 2011).

Illustration 3: The Online Academy of Irish Music

The Online Academy of Irish Music (OAIM) represents a departure from the other two illustrations in its medium of technology-based interaction, thereby recognising the need to reflect this growing culture of musical engagement. It is an Irish

---

7 Local government in Ireland comprises 31 local authorities. Limerick City and County Council has a multi-functional role of delivering services in such areas as housing, roads, transportation and planning as well as the arts service. See www.limerick.ie.

8 The Learning Hub (www.learninghub.ie) is a registered charity with the aim of working in partnership with local education providers, families and young people in Limerick city.

9 Co. Limerick is the 10th largest county in Ireland. Along with Limerick city as the only city in the county, it holds a population of approximately 191,000.

10 Limerick City and County Council is the local government administrative authority where the arts office is one of the Council's many services. See http://www.limerick.ie.

traditional music web-based platform for delivering Irish traditional music tuition online. Exploring in-depth this one online musical community, the OAIM (www. oaim.ie) rests within a broad constellation of online musical communities rooted in the Irish traditional music genre. The OAIM is one such online community among others which range from music video-sharing initiatives such as LiveTrad to internet sharing forums such as 'The session'. The OAIM is a subscription site where 'basic membership' can be gained for free to browse the site with limited access to 'sample lessons' ('tasters' of the video tutorials). A 'full access subscription' incurs monthly fees, which gives unrestricted access to the website and its resources. The OAIM is founded and managed by a couple living in Clare who bring in specialist expertise when needed, such as accountants and web-designers.

Although an online initiative, the physical location of the OAIM is also of interest to this case. The OAIM office is situated in County Clare, on the west coast of Ireland. Due to this location, the OAIM received a grant from the Clare County Enterprise Board (CEB)[11] in 2010 which paid for 50% of the start-up website costs. The location of the OAIM office also reflects a strong culture of Irish traditional music in this part of Ireland. Co. Clare is home to many well-known Irish traditional music legends (such as Willy Clancy and Micko Russell), music performers (such as the Kilfenora Céilí Band, Sharon Shannon and Martin Hayes) and festivals (such as the annual Willie Clancy Festival in Miltown Malbay and the Fleadh Nua in Ennis).

Structure of the book

The book is divided into three parts. Part I, 'a place for communities of musical practice', provides a conceptual and methodological framework for the book Chapter 1 explores key concepts of 'community', 'practice' and 'musical' within music education and relevant research fields. A discussion of issues and dilemmas surrounding CoMPs are mapped onto sub-themes of musical participation, identity and creativity. Locating itself within a sociocultural theoretical framework within the broader field of music education research, the scope and limitations of the community of practice framework are examined. Chapter 2 discusses the community of practice framework as a means to examine musical communities and outline the methodological choices taken to examine collective music-making. In its exploration of CoMPs, which relate to musical practices in differing contexts and genres with multiple viewpoints and sociocultural backgrounds, a conversation around the best means to capture and analyse both group and individual perspectives ensues.

Part II provides illustrations of CoMPs from the research sites. Chapters 3, 4 and 5 present an analysis of the practices of the adult amateur Limerick Jazz

---

11 Clare County Enterprise Board was one of 35 government-funded enterprise boards in Ireland which aimed to promote and develop small and medium-enterprise sectors in regional areas. See www.clareceb.ie. It was renamed LEO (Local Enterprise Office) Clare in 2014.

Workshop, County Limerick Youth Choir and Online Academy of Irish Music respectively. Each set of practices is evidenced from both group and individual perspectives. The examinations are divided thematically into community, musical and distinctive practices. Insights into each group's *modus operandi* are discussed drawing from observations, video data, participant logs and interviews, in addition to online forums in the case of the online community. In capturing the voices of these groups through the use of varied qualitative research methods, the analysis presented is rooted in micro practices but is located within the broader macro framework of group music-making contexts.

The final section of the book, Part III, offers insights and conclusions informed by the research. A comparison of the three CoMPs examined – the jazz, choral and online communities – is presented in Chapter 6. This discussion illuminates significant relationships, issues and themes across all three communities to draw together insights into the development of musical communities more broadly. Commonalities and differences shed new light on contemporary debates about how, why and where people learn music together. Chapter 7 considers the nature of CoMPs and their potential for transformation in music education. The power of CoMPs as a rich music education resource and sustainable model for musical participation is particularly highlighted. Thus, recommendations for fostering CoMPs are put forward in this final chapter with specific reference to both policy and practice. It is argued that there is a need to expand a view of music education to take account of these multiple and overlapping CoMPs that occur in local communities, cyberspace and across society.

Part I
A place for communities of musical practice

1 Defining communities of musical practice

The term 'communities of musical practice' (CoMPs) extends the notion of 'communities of practice' (CoPs), coined by the work of Lave and Wenger (1991) and Wenger (1998, 2006, 2002, 2000, 2009), to musical communities. The CoP framework offers a lens for conceptualising, understanding and analysing the development of music communities in practice. Wenger defines CoP as (2015) 'groups of people who share a concern or a passion for something they do and learn how to do it better as they interact regularly'. A link between learning and participation is put forward using three foundational dimensions: mutual engagement (domain), joint enterprise (process/community) and shared repertoire (practice) (1998, pp. 70–3). These three dimensions are fundamentally viewed as a sociocultural learning process where CoPs are constituted as holding varying levels of shared expertise, fluid membership roles that span from 'legitimate peripheral participation' to 'expert' and a shared purpose within a domain of knowledge. In investigating CoMPs, focusing on the ways that distinct communities make meaning from and interpret their shared music-making experiences shape and underpin this book.

Community perspectives

The connection between music and community bears particular relevance to CoMPs. The local music practices presented through research share insights into the musical and social interactions involving rules, learning, values, relationships and identities within communities. Wenger (2002, p. 38) describes 'community' as 'a group of people who interact, learn together, build relationships and in the process develop a sense of belonging and mutual commitment'. This definition sits alongside a conceptualisation of learning as 'situated' (Lave & Wenger, 1991); where knowledge is context-specific, occurring through one's environment and lived experiences. In this sense, music-making and musical learning cannot be divorced from context.

'Situated learning' or 'authentic learning' specifically takes up the idea of the acquisition of knowledge through participation in sociocultural contexts (Koopman, 2007; Lave & Wenger, 1991). The book, underpinned by such worldviews, investigates an ontological question of what the nature of 'situated learning' is as it occurred within the CoMPs investigated. Epistemologically, the research examines learning and meaning-making processes within the CoMP's collective musical and social practices. This sociocultural lens draws heavily on the work of Vygotsky (1962; Vygotsky & Cole, 1978, 1993) and Bruner (1990, 1996) where learning is conceived as embedded within social events and interactions. For Vygotsky, learning is viewed as 'situated action' within a 'zone of proximal development' which allows for varying levels of expertise and skills within groups where apprenticeship or peer learning is encouraged. Bruner extends this 'scaffolding' and 'mediational' approach to learning by emphasising knowledge building that is context-specific within a 'community of mutual learners' (1996, p. 24). He explains (1996, p. 21): 'it models ways of doing or knowing, provides opportunity for emulation, offers running commentary, provides "scaffolding" for novices, and even provides a good context for teaching deliberately'. Through such learning communities, Bruner asserts, 'reality is made, not found' (1996, p. 19) and as such knowledge is jointly constructed. So if learning occurs from and with others, as members of communities, the assumption is that within CoMPs the building of collective knowledge will be key to musical learning.

Within the field of music education, there has been a growing concern in what Folkestad (2006, p. 136) views as 'a general shift in focus –from teaching to learning, and consequently from teacher to learner'. Due to this shift, examining *where* music learning occurs and *how* it occurs has meant an increased focus on 'local' music or 'community music' research (Bennett, 2000; Cohen, 1991; Cottrell, 2004; Duffy, 2000; Finnegan, 2007; Higgins, 2007, 2012; Shuker, 2008; Slobin, 1993; Veblen, 2004; Veblen, Messenger, Silverman, & Elliott, 2013). Lee Higgins focuses on 'community music' as encapsulating a 'participatory ethos', with a focus on group participation emphasising a preoccupation with equality and access to music experiences (2007, pp. 282–4). Higgins is quite explicit in linking 'community music' to an act of 'cultural democracy' where (2012, p. 7) 'musicians who work within it are focussed on the concerns of making and creating musical opportunities for a wide range of people from many cultural groups'. Veblen and Olsson describe 'community music' in more broad, holistic terms, describing it as 'active participation in music-making of all kinds' (2002, p. 730). Similarly Blanford and Duarte (2004, p. 7) refer to it as 'any collective music-making activity initiated by members of the community'.

Although 'community music' is often associated as an activity outside of educational institutions, Ruth Finnegan recognises both formal and informal settings (casual, unregulated) as being a dynamic part of the 'musical worlds' she encountered in Milton Keynes where (2007, p. 206) 'schools are something more than just channels to lay the foundation for "proper" musical participation in later life; they are *themselves* organised centres of music – a real part of local musical practice'. Allsup (2003, 2012), Folkestad (2006), and Finney and Philpott (2010) also warn that the perceived dichotomy between formal and informal music learning is false (regardless of context). Allsup writes of 'stark binaries between out-of-school music and in-school music (2012, p. 181) and Folkestad advocates that music learning should be regarded as 'two poles of a continuum' (2006, p. 135).

Taking these views, 'musicians constantly learn music in this way in all traditions i.e. in a dialectic between the formal and informal' (Finney & Philpott, 2010, p. 9). The concept of 'non-formal' learning has also been incorporated into music education discourses (Coffman, 2002; Mok, 2011; Veblen, 2012) where much community music-making can be understood in this way. Here, the focus is on learning through group interaction guided by a teacher/facilitator/leader. Taking these views, the book observes the varied and overlapping practices of formal, informal and non-formal ways of musical learning within CoMPs and examines how and where such learning occurs.

One of the illustrations from practice presented in the book is an online CoMP. The inclusion of one such community in the study reflects this new fast-growing environment for musical learning and practice. The online nature of such communities expands the notion of 'community' and 'practice'. 'Online communities' can be defined, according to Plant (2004, p. 54) as 'a collective group of entities, individuals or organisations that come together either temporarily or permanently through an electronic medium to interact in a common problem or interest space'. It is important to note here that the emphasis remains on 'a collective'.

The CoP framework sits quite well in relation to online communities. It is argued, 'Technology extends and reframes how communities organise and express boundaries and relationships, which changes the dynamics of participation, peripherality and legitimacy' (Wenger et al., 2009, p. 11). Extending the concept of CoPs, such online 'musical worlds' (Finnegan, 2007) could also be conceptualised as 'digital habitats' (Wenger, White, & Smith, 2009, p. 38) where 'members have developed to take advantage of the technology available and thus experience this technology as a "place" for community'.

Increasingly, studies are focusing on the relationship between musical communities and online developments in recent years (Burnard, 2009; Kenny, 2013a, 2013b; Kibby, 2000; Partti & Karlsen, 2010; Ruthmann & Hebert, 2012; Salavuo, 2006; Waldron, 2009, 2011, 2013; Waldron & Bayley, 2012; Webster, 2011). Such online communities present a new form of musical engagement and participation within society that might on the face of it appear as a shift away from the study of 'local' musical communities to 'global' musical communities. Yet, in Kibby's study of a popular musician's chat page, she finds 'a virtual place that facilitated the belief in a local music community' (Kibby, 2000, p. 100). Furthermore, this study shows that the presence of an online 'place' did not necessarily translate into an automatic 'community' but rather, in a similar way to face-to face communities, 'communities exist through dialogue; through an exchange of past social history and current social interaction' (Kibby, 2000, p. 91).

Practice perspectives

Within the CoP model, Wenger characterises 'practice' as (2002, p. 38) 'socially defined ways of doing things in a specific domain: a set of common approaches and shared standards that create a basis for action, communication, problem solving, performance and accountability'. This notion of 'practice' clearly draws influence from the sociocultural theories of Bourdieu (Bourdieu, 1977, 1984, 1990, 2002; Bourdieu & Johnson, 1993). Bourdieu presents 'fields of practice' as a 'field of forces' (Bourdieu, 2002, p. 230) where the social and economic interactions of aesthetic experience are played out across social classes. Within this concept 'ways of doing' are generated through structures and interactions to acquire 'habitus' – a set of beliefs, dispositions, attitudes and practices. For the purposes of this book, 'habitus' is developed, negotiated and sustained through participation within CoMPs. Put simply, 'practices are things we do and develop', writes Burnard (2012a, p. 266), to acquire a 'feel for the game' (Bourdieu & Johnson, 1993).

According to Bourdieu, knowledge is gained through participation in a social world through the integration of agent, world and activity (1977, 1990). Lave and Wenger further expand this view of social practice, claiming (1991, p. 51):

> learning, thinking and knowing are relations among people in activity in, with, and arising from the socially and culturally structured world. This world is socially constituted; objective forms and systems of activity, on one hand, and agents' subjective and intersubjective understandings of them, on the other, mutually constitute both the world and its experienced forms.

Relating this to the CoMP investigated then, the 'world' relates to the social, cultural, geographic, economic and political framework, 'agent' to the actual actors or members of the CoMP and activity indicating the actual practice, discipline or domain involved – in this study, musical practices.

There has been a repeated call to engage with a more nuanced understanding of music sociology beyond Bourdieu (Born, 2010; DeNora, 2003; Prior, 2011; Wolff, 2008). Wolff argues for a shift to 'post-critical aesthetics' where notions of beauty within aesthetic experience are reconnected with the situated nature of engagements (2008). Prior similarly notes, 'not all aesthetic processes can be reduced to questions of power, symbolic exclusion and institutional process' (2011, p. 125). Much of the criticism stems from Bourdieu's deterministic view of art objects (including music) as manifestations of social forces as opposed to artistic forces. DeNora's (2003) arguments for a 'sociology with music' (as opposed to a 'sociology of music') emphasise the need for researchers to attend to how music matters to groups who make it. While Bourdieu's concepts have been useful to this research, then, the research uses various theoretical perspectives to inform its directions and discussions.

The influential writings of de Certeau in 'The Practice of Everyday Life' (1984) have interesting insights for a consideration of CoMPs. Akin to Bourdieu's theory of 'habitus', de Certeau discusses 'formalities of practices' and 'operational schema' (1984, pp. 29–30) as 'ways of operating' which conform to certain 'rules'. De Certeau's views on 'place' and 'space' are also useful. Using an example of a city street, 'space' is put forward as a place in practice (de Certeau, 1984, p. 117) whereby its walkers transform a street from a 'place' to a 'space'. In this way, policies can decide on the 'places' where they wish to support music communities but it is the music community themselves and the operations within it that create a 'space' for a potential CoMP to develop.

The praxial philosophies of David Elliott offer thought-provoking parallels to the concepts of 'practice' and 'habitus' as they are rooted in the idea of music as action or 'doing' (Elliott, 1995; Elliott, 2005; Elliott & Silverman, 2014). It is claimed, 'musical action and musical context work together to co-produce musical understanding' (Elliott, 1995, p. 61). 'Musical practice' is regarded as social practice that is context-bound within this praxial view of music. In this way, the music-making within CoMPs cannot be separated from their social and cultural contexts. The emphasis on practice particularly makes the CoP model an appropriate framework for the study. Davies (2005, p. 560) asserts, 'The core of the community of practice concept resides in the importance of *doing* . . . it is about local meanings, and individuals' management of their identities'.

Ethnomusicologist John Blacking discusses the use of the term 'music' and 'musical' by relating how musical processes generate music products (1995, pp. 148–68). Taking his view of a 'musical community' (p. 168), this book too chooses the term 'communities of *musical* practice' as opposed to *music* practice for its emphasis on process and practices as distinct to music outputs. While music outputs may result from such musical practices, the importance of the communal process is elevated here. Elliott explains (Elliott, 2007, p. 85), 'music involves sonic products, but these are created, maintained, adapted, reinterpreted, and appropriated by people in and across musical communities. Accordingly, music and our perceptions of it are always artistic/social/cultural/political/communal— and more'.

As well as this, the term 'communities of musical practice' is the most common version used in literature when linking music with a 'community of practice' framework (Barrett, 2003; 2005b; Campbell, 2002; Harwood, 1998; Kenny, 2014b; Marsh, 1995) and so ensures consistency across music education discourses. Encapsulating the key concepts put forward then, Figure 1.1 presents a working definition of CoMPs for the book.

Scope and limitations of the framework

The CoP concept (Lave & Wenger, 1991; Wenger, 1998) as a way to understand communities outside of workplaces has been limited and is frequently used as a mechanism for improving organisational effectiveness. The CoP model has been used by some music education researchers, however, although to a limited degree (Barrett, 2005a; Beineke, 2013; Blair, 2008; Burwell, 2012; Countryman, 2009; Froehlich, 2009; Gaunt & Dobson, 2014; Karlsen, 2010; Kenny, 2014b; Partti & Karlsen, 2010; Pellegrino, 2010; Waldron, 2009). Taking an instrumental case study approach of one CoMP, I previously used the CoP framework to examine a community-university partnership project (Kenny, 2014b). It was found that the framework is highly appropriate to bring to light the inter-relatedness of musical and social interaction within such an analysis as well as providing a focused interpretive lens with which to discuss data findings. It emerged that the

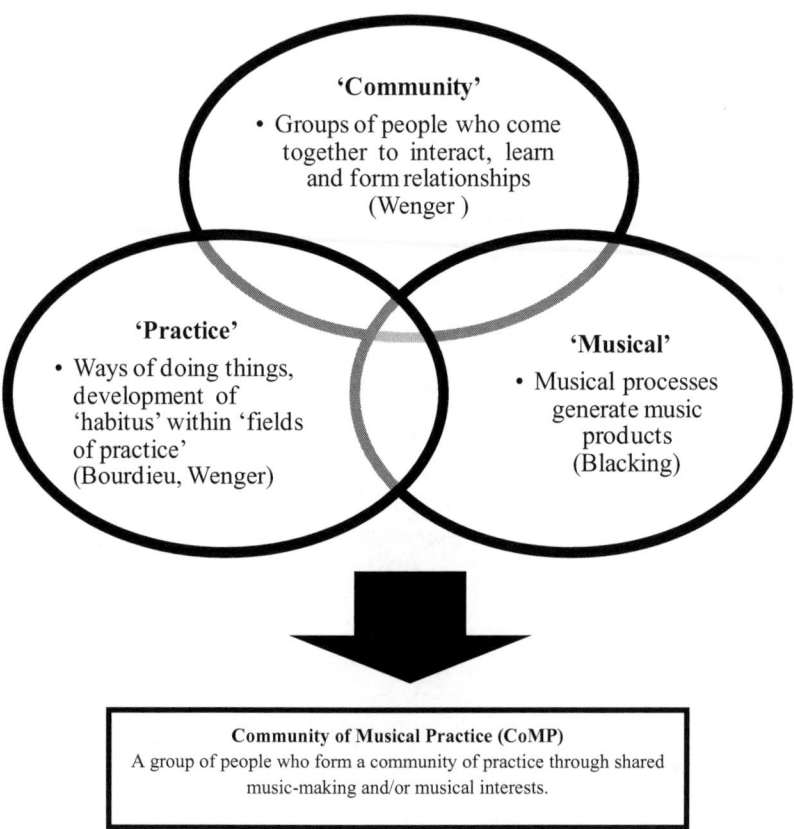

Figure 1.1 Summary of key concepts and definition of CoMP

framework led to an informed understanding during analysis of how this particular musical community interacted, learned, formed relationships, participated, made meaning and constructed knowledge.

Margaret Barrett in examining children's musical cultures (2005a) refers to 'children's communities of musical practice'. Through its application Barrett aimed to gain 'a greater understanding of children's musical cultures, and the ways in which musical meanings are negotiated within these cultures' (2005a, p. 190). It was found that children were 'active social agents' (2005a, p. 261) in their learning within CoMPs and Barrett called for the need to cultivate communities of practice within music education, where more vertical, didactic pedagogical approaches prevail. She claims (Barrett, 2005a, p. 275), 'One of the challenges for music education lies in generating the positive dimensions of a community of practice in an environment where the distinguishing elements of a community of practice would appear to be oppositional to the prevailing norms and practices of the institutional setting'. Barrett recommends more open, participatory approaches to music education, where learning is designed collaboratively, takes account of the broader environment and value systems, and is seen as a 'life-long' journey of musical learning (2005a, pp. 275–6).

In a series of case studies of high school music programmes in Canada (Countryman, 2009), the CoP framework was employed as an analytical tool. Countryman found that operationalising the CoP model provided 'nuanced and fluid vehicles for learning' (2009, p. 96) during data analysis. Countryman coded interview transcripts three times in three different ways and found the most beneficial analysis was when using the CoP triumvirate model (mutual engagement, joint enterprise and shared repertoire): 'Exploring the theoretical tenets of the concept "community of practice" helped me to interpret this differentiated experience of community' (Countryman, 2009, p. 98). Where the three dimensions of mutual engagement, joint enterprise and shared repertoire were present, the music programmes were perceived as 'transformative', 'fun' and promoted further musical participation into adulthood as opposed to those who experienced a 'rehearsal model' in music programmes.

An examination of a higher music education programme for rock musicians in Sweden (BoomTown) also used the CoP framework for analysis (Karlsen, 2010). This two-year programme based its pedagogical philosophy around the CoP framework whereby the need for authenticity through sociocultural learning process was all-important. Findings from the study indicate that the programme was essentially an 'educational community of practice' that bridged both formal and informal learning processes through such components as apprenticeship learning, engaging with members socially and musically, and informing identity through membership.

Bourdieu's focus on the 'position' of 'agents' (2002) has parallels with Lave and Wenger's (1991) focus on membership. Lave and Wenger put forward the concept of 'legitimate peripheral participation' and 'apprenticeship' as central to the CoP framework where membership is constantly evolving to move from peripheral to full participation through engagement in practice. In this way legitimate peripheral participation is viewed as 'a way of understanding learning' where learning is improvised, changing and wholly dependent on participation and membership within a CoP. Participation in particular is viewed as 'a way of learning – of absorbing and being absorbed in – the "culture of practice"' (Lave & Wenger, 1991, p. 91).

Membership within a CoP varies from full participation to peripheral participation and marginal participation (Wenger, 1998). Within this apprenticeship model of learning, 'newcomers' learn from 'oldtimers' within the community who are seen to hold 'expert knowledge' (Lave & Wenger, 1991; Wenger, 1998). There have been criticisms of this model highlighting issues of access and exclusion (Barton & Tusting, 2005; Benzie, Mavers, Somekh, & Cisneros-Cohernour, 2005; Fuller, Hodkinson, Hodkinson, & Unwin, 2005). Davies notes (2005, p. 566), 'Essentially, it must be a question of sanction: some individuals are allowed their choice of participation . . . whereas others are marginalized'. Wenger acknowledges that CoPs can breed 'toxic coziness' (Wenger et al., 2002, p. 144) and so diversity is key to sustaining fluid and changing CoPs (1998, pp. 75–6):

'Each participant in a community of practice finds a unique place and gains a unique identity, which is both further integrated and further defined in the course of engagement in practice'.

In later writings, Wenger (2006) emphasises 'individual learning trajectories' within CoPs where membership is viewed as a journey dependent on 'identity, passion, relationships, and a mutual commitment to a domain of knowledge' (2006, p. 36). This paradigm shift for education rejects a mass production of skills in favour of a customised vision of learning where personal engagement and identity transformation within communities are developed. Thus, society is viewed as a social learning system, where 'horizontalization' (peer-to-peer learning) enables individuals to make meaning and find their 'place' within communities.

The three dimensions of Wenger's criteria for CoPs are summarised below in Table 1.1 in relation to the study in this book.

Table 1.1 Wenger's criteria for CoP (1998) in relation to the study

Criteria for CoP	Description	Study
Mutual engagement (domain)	This explains the actual domain where regular interaction and sets of relationships form a common endeavour. Regular interaction is required for mutual engagement to develop.	The mutual engagement for CoMPs is the music-making group interactions such as rehearsals, workshops and performances. The relationships, interactions and negotiated meanings between the members are of relevance here as these are what essentially build the CoMP.
Joint enterprise (process)	Related to the process itself, this encapsulates the interactions, shared goals and negotiation that CoPs entail. Wenger describes this aspect as 'all the energy they spend' (1998, p. 78). It involves stated goals, negotiated goals and mutual accountability through collective practice. An appreciation of context is also required here.	Stated and negotiated aims of the music communities are relevant here. How the members problem-solve in response to the local context and situations negotiates the CoMP enterprise.
Shared repertoire (practice)	This describes the actual practice, seen as shared ways of doing, joint pursuit and communal resources that make and negotiate meaning. Such indicators as stories, routines, gestures, jokes or conversations build on a history of mutual engagement to build these practices.	Within the CoMP explored, this consists of the practices or built-up communal resources that distinctly belong to each musical community. They use these practices to negotiate meaning through practice.

This book extends the use of a CoP framework within musical communities and examines its potential as a means of analysing and interpreting 'situated' and collaborative musical practice. Key questions and concepts of community (where do we belong?), identity (who are we becoming?), practice (what are we doing?) and meaning (what is our experience?) also underpin and inter-relate with the three dimensions of CoPs. These concepts are employed as 'thinking tools' (Burnard, 2012b) within a broad analytical framework of the study.

Communities of practice and music education

Through an examination of CoMPs, important issues of musical participation, collaboration, identity and creativity are problematised as socio-musical practices. These salient themes are explored frequently throughout the book and so varying perspectives are considered here in relation to them.

Musical participation and collaboration

Due to an increased interest in researching music education in informal contexts, 'musical participation' as a field has enjoyed particular focus in recent years (Burnard, 2012b; DeNora, 2000; Finnegan, 2007; Green, 2002; Lamont, 2011; Pitts, 2005, 2012; Turino, 2008). Finnegan's ethnographical work on local music in Milton Keynes in the 1980s exerted much influence on this field of research. Finnegan puts forward an idea of 'musical worlds' or 'pathways' (2007) to describe the various forms of musical participation she encountered, describing these 'musical worlds' as (2007, p. 32):

> distinguishable not just by their differing musical styles but also by other social conventions: in the people who took part, their values, their shared understandings and practices, modes of production and distribution, and the social organisation of their collective musical activities.

Minnette Mans extends this notion of 'musical worlds' in her work as a 'conceptual and practical organisation of sound, movement, meaning, values, and rules' (2009, p. 5). Akin to Finnegan, she emphasises musical practice as encompassing both individual and collective musical participation rooted within cultural contexts.

In a study of local, amateur rock bands in Liverpool, Sarah Cohen (Cohen, 1991, 1994) similarly discovered a deep connection between musical, cultural and social practice within musical participation where the bands were rooted to context, creating a distinct 'Liverpool sound'. Hildegard Froehlich, employing a symbolic interactionist lens, has often written about the 'connectedness' and 'webs of interaction' involved in building community relationships within contexts through musical endeavour (2009, 2015). She argues that all collective musical acts involve dialogic learning where musical knowledge goes through a process of re-contextualisation (2015). Christopher Small shares a similar view of music education as social practice (1998, p. 208):

The big challenge to music educators today seems to me to be not how to produce more skilled professional musicians but how to provide that kind of social context for informal as well as formal musical interaction that leads to real development and to the musicalizing of the society as a whole.

This 'musicalizing' of society promotes the value of musical participation as a path to musical learning. For Small the meaning of music does not lie in the end product or performance itself, but rather in what people do and how they participate through music-making. In particular, Small sees this 'musicalizing' to be wholly dependent on building relationships through musical participation.

This notion of building relationships through music-making where music is considered as part of social life is also advocated by Thomas Turino (2008). Turino writes of music-making (2008, p. 18), 'We are fully focussed on an activity that emphasises our *sameness* – of time sense, of musical sensibility, of musical habits and knowledge, of patterns of thought and action, of spirit, of common goals – as well as our direct interaction'. This 'sonic bonding' or 'seamless synchrony' (Turino, 2008, p. 19) emphasises the socio-musical relationships involved in musical participation. Turino writes of the struggles of 'local music' gaining little or no media attention which he claims has a significant valuable effect on people and places where 'People develop a deeper sense of engagement and investment through direct participation in contrast to simply being a spectator or consumer' (2008, p. 231).

Bowman writes of the constitutive nature of the relationship between the social and musical, putting forward the notion of 'we' as central to musical practices (2007, p. 109):

> At the center of all music making and musical experience lies a 'we,' a sense of collective identity that powerfully influences individual identity. 'I am,' then, not so much because 'I think' or because 'I perceive,' but because 'we are,' and more particularly I want to assert here, because 'we are, musically'.

Emphasising the ethical dilemmas of inclusion and exclusion within such a musical 'we', Bowman highlights the complexity within such musical communities where 'musical exclusions then, are always also exclusions of people' (Bowman, 2007, p. 118). Bradley similarly questions the development of community within music-making as an assumed 'common good'. She claims (Bradley, 2009, p. 57), 'striving to develop musically a sense of community always and already runs the risk of the development of its fascistic forms'. Examining powerful, collective 'musical moments' as potential sites for manipulation, Bradley calls on a need for ongoing reflexivity to interrogate musical participation within communities. It is vitally important within our fields of research then to challenge our often taken-for-granted assumptions about the benefits within (and outside of) musical communities.

Recent writings from Pitts (2012) on the long-term effects of music education on adults' engagement, attitudes and involvement in music also raise important questions about how people are taught music and why they continue to participate in musical experiences. Through 'life histories' it was found that opportunities to experience music in school, community and home settings were vital to immediate engagement and long-term interest in music. Speaking of experiences outside of classrooms, Pitts states, 'the emotional richness embedded in the descriptions of extra-curricular music is striking: rehearsals, concerts, repertoire, and personalities are recalled much more vividly than classroom experiences of music' (2012, p. 66). While impact was deemed to be not directly predictable, the research found that lack of musical participation opportunities often limited future ambitions to make music.

Musical participation can also lead to a strong sense of 'belonging' among members of musical communities. In her authoritative examination of musical participation across four case studies, Pitts relates (2005, p. 53), 'Making music with others was shown to affirm a sense of belonging and like-minded endeavour, so sustaining commitment and offering a shared experience that fostered memories and friendships among a diverse group of people'. Whether it was performers at an opera festival or participants in a contemporary music summer school, it is clear from the study that 'collective musical endeavour' (whether through performance or rehearsal) allowed participants to establish 'a network of experiences that buil[t] or reinforce[d] their sense of being musically active and engaged' (Pitts, 2005, p. 71). Such experiences through musical participation also emerged as a significant influence on identity formation.

In an action research study of a high school choral ensemble, Elizabeth Parker writes (2010, p. 344), 'participants expressed that chorus represents an even playing field where everyone contributes towards the whole. They work in collaboration with one another to support the larger ensemble'. The study relates that singing itself in the choir created the medium for 'belonging'; facilitating a shared experience, 'safe space' and identity of an 'in-group'. Sectional bonding within the choir (grouped by voice type) is seen to promote 'social bonding' (Parker, 2010) and in a further study of adolescent choral singing findings reveal that, 'Through the act of singing with others, involvement in choir reaches beyond membership into belonging and peak experiences' (Parker, 2014, p. 28). Similarly, Power (2010), in an investigation of community singing, writes of 'social bonding' where through interviews with two choirs it emerges, 'participants never lost sight of the gathering that happens in rehearsals as a social event as well as a learning event' (2010, p. 9).

In her examination of 'natural voice' and 'world song', Caroline Bithell shares (2014, p. 224):

> Choir leaders and members regularly speak of the way in which their choir comes to represent a kind of family, one where members can experience a strong sense of togetherness and find friendship and support without needing to know a great deal about one another.

Drawing on social capital theories, Bithell argues that through the act of singing with others in inclusive, participatory 'community choirs', there is enormous potential for transformation to occur – at individual, communal and wider societal levels. As such, group singing becomes a political act, echoing writings from Karen Ahlquist's 'Chorus and Community' (2006). Through this series of diverse case studies, this edited collection also highlights the dual nature of 'belonging' both musically and socially within choirs, 'as music and as people' (2006, p. 1).

'Collaboration' through participation is an area that has also gained continued research focus (Barrett, 2005a, 2011; Berliner, 1994; Green, 2002; John-Steiner, 2000; Miell & Littleton, 2004; Sawyer, 2003, 2006b). Moran and John-Steiner define collaboration as (2004, p. 11) 'an intricate blending of skills, temperaments, effort and sometimes personalities to realise a shared vision of something new and useful'. Becker in his view of 'art worlds' believes that 'collective action' is an integral part of such collectives (2008, p. 34): 'Art worlds consist of all the people whose activities are necessary to the production of the characteristic works which that world, and perhaps others as well, define as art'. Sawyer too characterises music as 'a collaborative practice' and 'a communicative activity' (2006a, p. 161).

In particular, Sawyer in his studies of jazz ensembles references interaction as 'musical conversations' where players communicate and learn through the 'language of jazz' (Sawyer, 2006a). This focus on collaboration as well as communication within jazz ensembles is a feature of such studies (Becker, 2008; Berliner, 1994; MacDonald & Wilson, 2005; Sawyer, 2003, 2006b; Seddon, 2005). For instance, Seddon and Biasutti (2009) and Seddon (2005) describe 'musical communication' for jazz groups as a means to explicitly and implicitly learn and negotiate the 'rules' of improvisatory performance. These rules are learned through collaborative practice, both musical and social. Through such learning, which Sawyer coins as 'collaborative emergence', jazz ensembles sustain themselves on the premise that the whole is greater than the sum of its parts (2003, p. 12). The jazz ensemble studied in this book offers particular insight into how creativity emerges from collaboration. These findings are discussed in depth elsewhere (Kenny, 2014a) where it is found that within the ensemble collaborative creativity is dependent on both strong leadership but also collective inputs built up through a history of shared experiences.

Musical identity

This book aims to provide an important 'window' into how CoMPs form, negotiate and project identities through socio-musical interactions. Taking the views of Finnegan (2007) and Pitts (2005, 2009), identity formation within the social world where one lives can be considerably enhanced through musical participation within communities. Pitts maintains that musical participation (2005, p. 30) 'contributes to the development of participants' identities, providing a particular context where their behaviour and social relations may flourish'. Similarly, Finnegan (2007, p. 32) describes this connection within the 'musical worlds' discovered: 'Musical practice is essentially *of* society, dependent on and expressed in all kinds of activities and settings . . . through which people both realise and transcend their social existence'.

Maxine Greene (1995, 2001) repeatedly writes of 'attending' within aesthetic experiences and 'noticing what there is to be noticed' for transformation to occur. With regard to musical communities, then, members require creative, challenging musical encounters for meaningful learning to happen, to in turn shape their identities. Greene presents convincing arguments about the potential for transformation through meaningful arts experiences (1995, 2001). She contends that knowledge is constructed through experience, but also in partnerships – through creating relational spaces for transformation, 'encounters with the arts do indeed make for connections in experience, for patterns and new orders never imagined before' (Greene, 2001, p. 114).

Moran and Steiner define identity as (2004, p. 11) 'how people form themselves through what activities and roles they chose to 'make their own'. Stephen Cottrell in his ethnographical study of professional musicians in London writes (2004, p. 83):

Playing in small groups seems to provide for many people the perfect balance, musically speaking, between self and society; between on the one hand, the cultivation of an individual musical voice and, on the other, the integration of this voice with other similar voices for the purposes of musical production.

Allsup in writing of the phenomenon of school bands in the USA shares, 'there is no subject called band that exists apart from its students and teachers and the interests that its students and teachers find and bring with them. In other words, band is both shareholder and subject of study' (2012, p. 185). Hence, an examination into CoMPs can be perceived as a means of exploring the link between music, the individual and the social world where one exists. Mans asserts that through 'culturally informed systems of musical thinking and creating' (2009, p. 10) 'we can trace our cultural and musical identities individually and collectively to such worlds' (2009, p. 5). Music then is regarded as the mediator between individual and collective identities within a wider social context.

The book 'Musical Identities' (MacDonald, Miell, & Hargreaves, 2002) marks a most significant contribution to this field of research. This work has shown both that music is important in identity, and that identities are important in music. Within a social constructionist viewpoint, musical identities are deemed to be constructed through musical activity. Accordingly, identities continually evolve and are negotiated within the contexts of musical experience (Hargreaves, Miell, & MacDonald, 2002). In a further study of musical identities among Scottish professional jazz musicians, MacDonald and Wilson highlight the mutual process of individual and collective identity formation (2005). This process is deemed to be in a constant state of negotiation where (2005, p. 413) 'this identity is important to continuing and participating in the music, it is negotiated (rather than shared) in the group context in relation to individual musical identities and the perceived dispositions of others'. As such, individual perspectives, abilities and values are positioned within the broader 'jazz community'.

The notion of identity negotiation within sociocultural contexts is taken up by Miell and Littleton in their study of musical collaboration and identity within a teenage band (2008). From an analysis of video-recorded band rehearsals, it emerges that through the band members' interactions they are engaged in a process of forming 'musical common knowledge' and thus a collective band identity. Miell and Littleton write (2008, p. 47):

> they continually construct, negotiate and re-negotiate a shared understanding of the qualities of their sound—a kind of 'musical common knowledge'. What is at work, then, are interdependent, mutually constitutive processes whereby a sense of the band's musical identity directly enters into appraisal of a song, with the 'sound' of a song resourcing or problematising the group's claim to a particular, distinctive musical identity.

The forming of a musical identity collectively is not just confined to music-making in groups. Juuti and Littleton (2010) in their study of musical identities among solo piano students found that despite these students entering a music academy to develop solo performance careers, their identities were still very much shaped by collective, interactive, sociocultural processes. They explain that these identity negotiations (Juuti & Littleton, 2010, p. 14) 'both construct and reflect the sociocultural communities of which [the music students] are part, and their values, history and culture'. Therefore, musical identity is mediated through negotiations within 'musical worlds' (Finnegan, 2007; Mans, 2009) which include numerous stakeholders and influences.

Forming and negotiating a musical identity is often associated with an 'in-group' and 'out-group status' (Turino, 2008, p. 106). Folkestad alludes to this formation as a sense of 'belonging' to a particular group, claiming music 'provides a means of defining oneself as an individual belonging to and allied with a certain group, and of defining others as belonging to other groups'(2002, p. 151). Just as a sense of 'belonging' was seen as essential to musical participation previously (Bithell, 2014; Parker, 2010; Pitts, 2005; Power, 2010), it also acts as a signal of identity to a musical community, as well as a means of defining others' musical identities or lack thereof.

Thus, 'belonging' is not always a positive aspect of musical communities as to feel a sense of 'belonging' may require others not to 'belong' (as seen from Bowman and Bradley's writings discussed earlier). With regard to issues of identity, Pitts found that in a study of extra-curricular musical participation among adolescents (2008, p. 13), 'not being involved can create doubts about musical competence and resentment towards those who are seen as denying access to involvement'. This findings resonate with those of Lamont (2002, 2003) who also found that children and young people who did not gain access to instrumental music lessons outside of school saw themselves as 'non-musicians', despite gaining general music education in school. Access and participation within musical communities outside of school environments were therefore crucial to forming a musical identity. Within adult musical communities these 'in-group' and 'out-group' musical identities are often associated with defining amateur and professional musician status. Merriam (1964) and Finnegan (2007) describe this identity negotiation as being along a complex continuum where 'professionalism seems to run along a continuum from payment in occasional gifts at one end to complete economic support through music at the other' (Merriam, 1964, p. 165).

Musical communities can often act as a mediator to project and inform national as well as local identities (Becker, 2008; Blacking, 1995; Cohen, 1991, 1994, 2007; Colley, Eidsaa, Kenny, & Leung, 2012; Duffy, 2000; Finnegan, 2007; Firth, 1993; Folkestad, 2002; Kenny, 2011, 2013a; McCarthy, 1999; O'Flynn, 2009; Slobin, 1993; Waldron & Bayley, 2012; Waldron & Veblen, 2008; Zuberi, 2001). As the research study is rooted in an Irish context, Benedict Anderson's theories of 'imagined communities' and 'nation-ness' are useful (Anderson, 1991). Anderson directly points to the 'imagined' nature of connecting with nationalism as 'profound emotional legitimacy'. Anderson states that within nations and such cultural activities as singing national anthems (1991, p. 224), 'the members . . . will never know most of their fellow-members, meet them or even hear of them, yet in the minds of each lives the image of their communion'. Cohen in writing about a distinct 'Liverpool sound' claims, 'The globalization of cultural forms has been accompanied by a localization of cultural identity and claims to authenticity, resulting in a tension or dialectic between the two trends' (1994, p. 133).

Within an era of arguably 'the globalization and commodification of Ireland and Irish culture' (Scahill, 2009), seen through such international phenomena as *Riverdance* and *Lord of the Dance*,[1] Irish traditional music in particular developed what Slobin describes as an 'affinity interculture' internationally (Slobin, 1993). O'Flynn comments on a modern 'renaissance' of Irish traditional music from the 1990s onwards where *Riverdance* was seen as a pivotal cultural phenomenon in this regard (2009, p. 39): 'Irishness itself came to be represented by a combination of sounds, images and movements that were at once contemporary, uniquely Irish and self-confident . . . a kind of Irishness-in-your-face'.

Online music communities also raise interesting issues in relation to identity formation and negotiation. Much like musical communities 'on the ground', I have found that online communities develop identities within their own distinctive practices and web contexts (Kenny, 2016): 'although the music may remain genre-specific, the online community negotiates and fashions distinct practices particular to their new web space'. Furthermore, a connection between music and national identity within online communities can be very strong despite the lack of geographical location (Kenny, 2013a, 2013b).

Partti and Karlsen (2010) through an ethnographic approach collected data through observations of the activities on the music website mikseri.net in Finland. Through compiling 'musical life stories', the development of both individual and collective identities is evident (2010, p. 374): 'Community members use

---

1 *Riverdance* and *Lord of the Dance*, originating in 1994 and 1996 respectively, became highly successful theatrical shows of Irish traditional music and dance, and continue to be performed around the world today.

the site, not just to share their music, but also to construct their music-related identities within a web-based reality'. Findings reveal that these 'music-related identities' are socially constructed and negotiated within the online music community through engaging in a joint interest in music practice, peer interaction and learning, and participating directly with the music itself. Waldron's (2009, p. 106) study of an online *Old Time* community echoed those of Partti and Karlsen where she discovers that, 'Individual identity informs the communal and vice versa. . . . Identity thus emerges through the experiences of the individual within the communal'. In this manner, it is found that online identities were very similar to offline ones and so function under similar norms and identity negotiations.

Musical creativity

Taking the view that musical participation and identity formation occur within sociocultural contexts, conceptions and research surrounding 'creativity' have interesting insights to offer this discourse. An explosion of creativity research has been occurring since the 1950s and with it followed an increased focus on musical creativity. Creativity is often defined as the ability to produce work that is 'novel' (Ochse, 1990; Sternberg & Lubart, 1999; Sternberg & Lubart, 1995). However, increasingly the term 'creativity' is employed to describe a multiplicity of processes as opposed to a particular product or outcome (Burnard, 2012b; Sawyer, 2006b).

Definitions of creativity in music have largely focused on the production of new objects, usually by the means of composition or improvisation (Cambell & Scott-Kassner, 1995; Durrant & Welch, 1995; Hickey, 2002; Webster, 1990). Humphreys (2006, p. 357) argues:

> The construct of creativity in music education should be expanded to encompass the entire array of creative activities practised by musicians everywhere – not just at the professional level, not just in art music, not just composition, and not just in the West.

Csikszentmihalyi (1996) puts forward a concept of 'situated creativity' where creativity is seen as occurring through the interaction between a person's thoughts and sociocultural context. Creativity is viewed as lying within the sociocultural relationship between person, domain and field and presented as a 'systems model' of creativity (Csikszentmihalyi, 1996), demonstrated in Figure 1.2:

Certain rules and conventions are necessary within the domain (e.g. Irish traditional music) for creativity to occur within this jointly constructed model. A field of experts, peers and an audience validate this creativity, particularly when dealing with musical performance, and so provide it with a sense of worth. The role of the individual is to offer the field and domain something that is 'creative'. When such creativity is at its peak, or 'optimal experience', individuals are believed to experience 'flow' (Csikszentmihalyi, 1996).

Csikszentmihalyi's work has influenced a 'contextualised' and 'collaborative' view of creativity within music research where the social processes of group

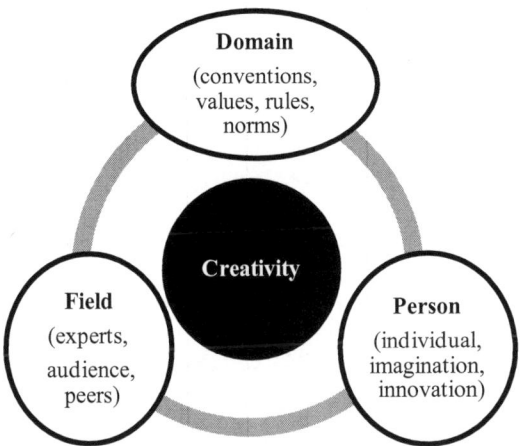

Figure 1.2 A 'systems model' of creativity (Csikszentmihalyi, 1996)

creativity are the focus (Burnard, 2006, 2012b; Custodero, 2012; Humphreys, 2006; Kenny, 2013c, 2014a; Miell & Littleton, 2004; Sawyer, 2003, 2006c). Burnard's work on 'musical creativities of practice' emphasises this sociocultural view of creativity (2012b). Through an examination of professional musicians varying from composers to singer-songwriters to DJs to bands, the multiplicity of various types of musical creativities are presented. Burnard builds on Csikszentmihalyi's 'systems model' (see Figure 1.2), and Bourdieu's conceptual tools (see earlier in this chapter), to reject linear or singular conceptions of musical creativity and instead offers a means of understanding the multiple sites of practice(s), relationships, modalities, systems, capitals and innovations that are involved in the practice of creativity.

This shift to characterising creative processes as dynamic, fundamentally social and collaborative emphasises creativity as a collective process. Sawyer defines characteristics of 'group creativity' as entailing: process, unpredictability, intersubjectivity, complex communication and emergence (2003, pp. 4–13). In studying jazz ensembles he views improvisation as 'the extreme case of group creativity' (2003, p. 13). When players are in the 'improvisation zone', Sawyer claims (2003, p. 41):

> groups attain flow by staying in the improvisation zone between complete predictability and going too far, between their shared knowledge about conventional situations, and doing something so inconsistent that it just doesn't make sense.

This correlates with findings from other jazz ensemble studies where the more experienced and familiar players are with each other and the deeper the domain of 'knowledge', the greater the levels of musical interaction, communication and creativity (Berliner, 1994; Csikszentmihalyi, 1996; Sawyer, 2003, 2006b; Seddon & Biasutti, 2009; Seddon, 2005). For example, Berliner describes such an outcome as 'striking a groove' (1994) while Seddon coins it is as 'empathetic attunement' where 'improvisers go beyond responding supportively to their fellow musicians and stimulate the conception of new ideas' (2005, p. 50).

These findings on group or collaborative creativity are not restricted to jazz ensembles. For instance, observations of children's musical creativity within the playground (Harwood, 1998; Marsh, 1995), within classrooms (Burnard, 2002, 2006; Young, 2003) and among students on higher education programmes (Kenny, 2013c, 2014b) point to the multiple locations for creativity to take place. Davidson and Good (2002) in their research on a string quartet claim 'spontaneous musical utterances' emerge from the 'interplay of stocks of musical knowledge'. Moran and John-Steiner write of the benefits of 'creative collaboration' as capitalising on the 'complementarity' and 'tensions' multiple perspectives, expertise and resources bring (John-Steiner, 2000; Moran & John-Steiner, 2003; 2004): 'Collaboration creates an environment where the partners can push the boundaries of themselves and integrate their differing personal characteristics' (Moran & John-Steiner, 2004, p. 21).

Such ideas on creativity are acutely relevant to this book in looking at creativity practices within the CoMP examined. Universally, there is a preoccupation with producing 'creative economies' (UNESCO, 2000, 2010, 2013) and the arts are seen to be a major player in this regard. Within Ireland, national, regional and local policy makers are increasingly using 'creativity' to justify and tailor arts support where the arts are being seen as a form of 'investment'. On a positive note, this has meant that the arts have received investment and status in their position to promote creativity. Laycock (2008, p. 72) writes, 'community arts . . . are about active participation in the creative process'. However, there are dangers in placing this form of 'value' on the arts, as John Tusa points out (2007, p. 164):

> For more and more is demanded of the arts, even as they get funded less and less. The government want the arts to make society richer; the Department of the Environment wants the arts to revive collapsed neighbourhoods; the Department for Education want the arts to fill the gaps in their own students' knowledge . . . the underlying fallacy is the belief that the arts can be the social and economic instruments without first being true to their own values.

The challenges of global and national pressures, fluctuating economic conditions, competing political agendas, multiple purpose initiatives and a need to show a return for public money all have direct implications on arts and music policy and in turn on musical practices. It is imperative therefore that future decisions and directions for music and arts development are sufficiently supported by best practice. Continued research into musical and broader arts communities are one such means to make certain that such practice is backed up by a strong researched knowledge base.

Summary

The book has aligned itself within a sociocultural theoretical framework where a definition of CoMPs is put forward to inform the study. Using this lens for the study, collective music-making is viewed as a social phenomenon which develops in particular contexts. Individuals participate within music communities to construct their own social realities and identities through musical and social interaction. Communities of practice are conceptualised and discussed in this chapter as a model for analysis and interpretation. The study then, in its examination of CoMPs as they exist within sociocultural, political, geographical and economic contexts, considers issues that surround socio-musical perspectives within this theoretical frame.

Musical participation is conceived in this chapter as rooted in sociocultural processes where relationships, a sense of 'belonging' and collaboration are revealed to be important to participants' musical experiences. Immersion in such 'musical worlds' (Finnegan, 2007; Mans, 2009) is related to form and inform musical identities. Whether online or offline, these musical identities are deemed to be negotiated on individual and collective levels through sociocultural contexts where the relationship between the music, individuals and society is crucial to identity formation.

An examination of musical creativity raises key questions for the research relating to how creativity is conceived, understood and observed within musical participation. In particular the 'situated' nature of creativity is highlighted. Research on 'collaborative creativity' and 'group creativity' is especially relevant to the examination of CoMPs where group music-making is investigated. Furthermore, the prevalent creativity policy discourse highlights some key issues on the dangers and affordances of such rhetoric.

2 Investigating communities of musical practice

A 'community of practice' (CoP) framework offers much potential for conceptualising, understanding and analysing the development of musical communities. This chapter discusses the framework as a means to examine such communities and outline the methodological choices taken to examine collective music-making within the Irish illustrations. The three communities of musical practice (CoMPs) examined in this book entail differing and multiple contexts, genres, viewpoints and sociocultural backgrounds. Thus, a discussion of the tools employed to capture, analyse and interpret both group and individual perspectives from these communities ensues.

Entering communities of musical practice

Operationalising the CoP model essentially involves focusing on the social process of learning within CoMPs for the selection, analysis and interpretation of the data. In the selection process for this study, *potential* CoMPs were identified based on an assumption that the three dimensions of mutual engagement (domain), joint enterprise (community) and shared repertoire (practice) (Wenger, 1998; Wenger, et al., 2002) were present. In addition, Wenger (1998, p. 125) provides a set of 14 indicators that form a CoP which include such aspects as: 'shared ways of engaging'; 'tools, representations and other artifacts'; 'local lore, shared stories, inside jokes'; and 'rapid flow of information and propagation of innovation'. *Actual* CoMPs were only determined during the analysis of the three case studies if the three fundamental elements and indicators were in fact present.

Studies that have used the CoP framework outside of music and music education research provide interesting insights. A study investigating a community of learners for vocational orientation combines the concepts of 'communities of learners' and 'communities of practice' for observations and interviews of teaching-learning processes in two pre-vocational secondary schools (Boersma, ten Dam, Volman, & Wardekker, 2010). This combination they felt offers the study 'a better theoretical understanding' (Boersma, et al., 2010, p. 4) and is employed to create four parameters to define their conceptualisation of a community of learners. While the focus of this article centres on the 'community of learners' theory, the combination of theory and use of a set of parameters to analyse the data is of relevance to this book where several sociocultural perspectives are drawn from (see Chapter 1). Further insight on using the CoP model as an analytic framework is provided by Benzie, Mavers, Somekh and Cisneros-Cohernour (2005) who in examining case studies in educational settings found the framework extremely useful to investigate issues of sociocultural learning processes such as situated meaning-making, identity formation, various levels of membership and notions of belonging.

In music education, the CoP model has also been employed as an analytical tool in various ways and degrees of depth as discussed in Chapter 1 (Barrett, 2005a; Beineke, 2013; Blair, 2008; Burwell, 2012; Countryman, 2009; Froehlich, 2009; Gaunt & Dobson, 2014; Karlsen, 2010; Kenny, 2014b; Partti & Karlsen, 2010; Pellegrino, 2010; Waldron, 2009). These studies highlight the potential of applying the CoP model to collective music-making activities and experiences. Building on this research, the power of the CoP model for conceptualising and interpreting data is important to the viability of the model to study musical communities.

The musical communities explored in this book are conceptualised in broader sociocultural, philosophical and epistemological views that go beyond the CoP framework, however. The CoP model therefore acts as a point of departure where other theories and literature relating to musical identity, collaboration, participation and creativity (discussed most specifically in Chapter 1) extend its use for examining group music-making.

The case study

A qualitative case study approach was identified as appropriate to the study as dealing with CoMPs involves an investigation into 'real life', 'ordinary', 'life experiences' (Bogdan & Biklen, 2007). A leading expert in case study research, Robert Yin, asserts (2009, p. 4), 'the distinctive need for case studies arises out of the desire to understand complex social phenomena'. In an attempt to address research questions relating to musical practices in differing contexts, genres, with multiple viewpoints and identities, a qualitative case study research design offered a means of capturing such complexities. Within a sociocultural learning framework, the selected 'cases' helped to illuminate the CoP model in practice and relate it to the 'real world' (Robson, 2002).

The unifying aspect of the selected communities was that they were all in some way government supported (for example through funding, accommodation, expertise, administration), located within the mid-west of Ireland and engaged in music-making. This 'bounded system' (Creswell, 2007a, p. 73) specifically involved Limerick city, County Limerick and one online community which had its office in County Clare (details of each research site are outlined within Chapter 1). The map in Figure 2.1 sets out the geographical context of the study nationally.

The case study could be further classified as a 'multiple-case study' (Yin, 2006, p. 113) but the term 'collective case study' was favoured due to its dominance in case study literature (Creswell, 2007b) and its suitability to describe the three 'cases' or communities to be studied in context. Using a collective case study approach, Stake asserts, 'understanding them will lead to better understanding,

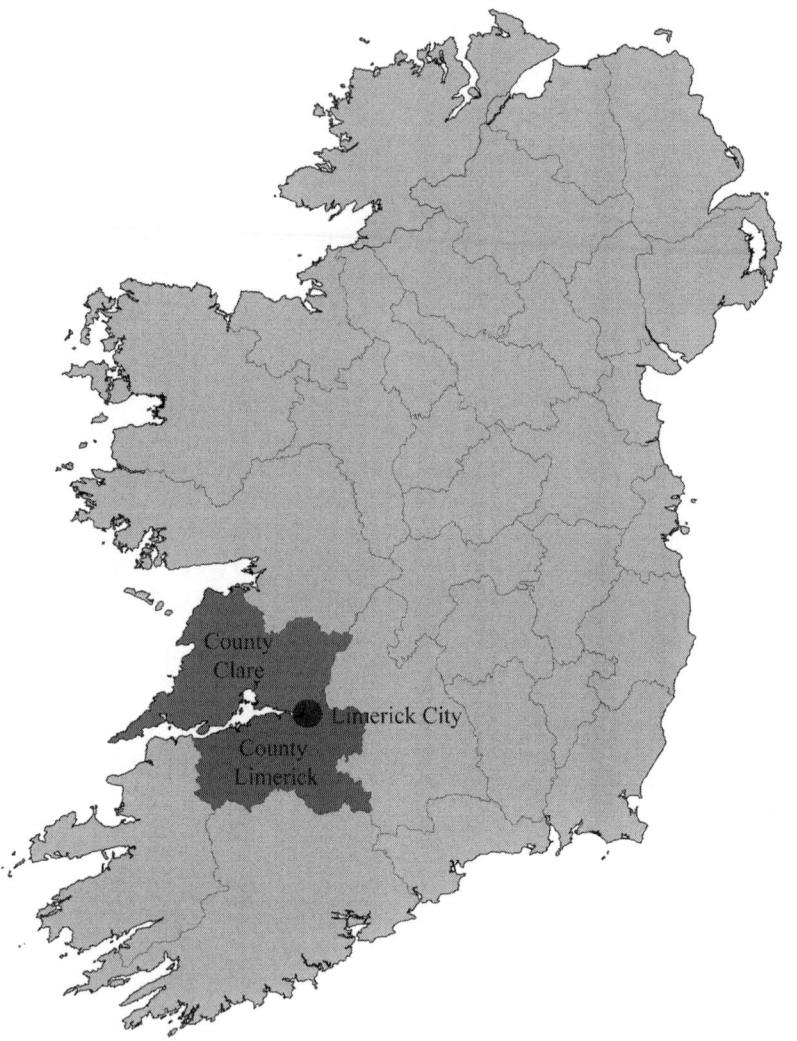

Figure 2.1 Map of Ireland and case study locations

perhaps better theorizing, about a still larger collection of cases' (Stake, 2000, p. 437). This is not to say that the cases can lead to hard and fast 'evidence', as Creswell warns: 'There are no right stories, only multiple stories' (2007b, p. 44). The research does not attempt to claim that the findings are generalisable outside of the actual settings themselves; however, conclusions drawn from the findings may claim to be theoretically generalisable and contribute to theory building (Yin, 2009). The study in its investigation of social phenomena was very much rooted within a broad theoretical framework outlined in Chapter 1.

Drawing lessons from other case studies was key to informing the research methodology and methods. A case study approach is used by Pitts in an examination of musical participation across four projects (2005). Each case is selected as an example of musical participation and in a similar manner to Finnegan (2007) in studying 'musical worlds' in Milton Keynes and Cottrell (2004) examining professional musicians in London, the case selection is based on personal experience and one geographical area around Sheffield. In a comparable fashion to the 'hidden musicians' study (Finnegan, 2007) the musical situations in the Pitts research are described in detail, compared and contrasted but with a specific focus on the role of music in individual lives. Mixed methods of questionnaires, interviews, diaries and fieldwork observations are employed in the study though not necessarily all being used for each of the four projects. Rather, in a pragmatic approach the methods are applied to suit each situation or context; a strategy that has also proved useful for consideration in this research.

Studies of band rehearsals and collective music-making (Littleton & Mercer, 2012; Miell & Littleton, 2008) also influenced the approaches to data collection and analysis in this book. In Miell and Littleton's investigation of teenage band rehearsals, members' talk and musical interactions are analysed through filmed rehearsals. The video data serves as a highly useful means to capture 'collaborative music-making' where 'valuable opportunities for collaborative learning and working are fortuitous, serendipitous and improvised' (2008, p. 47). An analysis of talk and joint musical activity from video data endeavours to capture the complexities of these musical and social interactions. The significance of employing video data to this research is discussed further in this chapter.

A case study approach allowed for extensive, varied data collection, had an identifiable 'bounded system' and most importantly, in fitting with the research objectives, allowed for an in-depth investigation and analysis of grounded, 'real-world' (including virtual world) experiences. In studying musical ensembles, Seddon and Biasutti argue (2009, p. 398), 'In order to investigate the communication that takes place between small groups of musicians during rehearsal and performance it is necessary to observe their activities and to have a method of analysis available to interpret their behaviours'. The use of several qualitative research methods within the study ensured triangulation where rigour, multiple perspectives and different types of data were all important to the validity of the study.

In seeking to understand 'musical worlds' (Finnegan, 2007; Mans, 2009) or from a sociocultural theory viewpoint, 'fields of practice' (Bourdieu, 2002, pp. 230–1), a purposive sample of three cases was selected. A collective case study of three CoMPs provided a balance and variety in (1) setting, (2) emerging and established communities, (3) children and adults, (4) professional and amateur musicians and (5) varied musical genres. The three cases are briefly outlined and described in Chapter 1.

The aim of electing three sites was based on those that offered the most 'opportunity to learn' (Stake, 2000, p. 447) about the development of and learning within CoMPs. The number of 'cases' to select for such an examination created several dilemmas. With a single case, a thoroughly in-depth, ethnographic study could ensue. However, such a study could prove to be idiosyncratic and threaten the validity and reliability of the study with respect to its more universal aims. A case study which selected *all* potential CoMPs in the mid-west of Ireland was also considered. From preliminary meetings with local government arts officers, it emerged that this approach could amount to hundreds of cases and so would no doubt be more suitable to a quantitative study. Such a study would serve to provide a broad outline of *what* existed in practice rather than relating to the *how and why* questions which were of more concern in this research. Thus, three cases were identified as suitable to create sufficient depth of analysis to address the research questions (see Introduction) while also providing three distinct illustrations into varying types of CoMPs to allow for interesting cross-comparisons.

The site and plethora of music communities selected went through a pre-fieldwork 'case study screening procedure' (Yin, 2006, p. 115). Personal as well as professional information and connections gathered information from both formal and informal meetings with academics, amateur and professional musicians, resource agencies as well as meetings with the local government arts officers around the mid-west of Ireland. From this, *potential* CoMPs were explored (using the three CoP dimensions as a guide), communities that receive government support identified, the willingness of key stakeholders/gatekeepers to participate probed and most importantly, the potential richness of data from various music communities ascertained. From this, each potential site was approached through a recognised leader and initial consent was granted before embarking on the research.

Examining communities of musical practice

Data collection occurred between October 2010 and June 2011. This time was spent 'in the field' across all three research sites as shown in Table 2.1. Using both a sequential and concurrent design (Creswell, 2007a; Creswell 2009), the research was split into three phases. The research methods gathered data from informal meetings, document analyses (over the first three months), video observations, online forums, participant logs (carried out over seven months) and interviews (in the last three months). The data was collected through a staggering process across all three 'cases' of the research timeline. In this manner the various data sets captured both group and individual insights into the workings of the CoMP selected.

Although the overlapping phases were especially laboursome, by converging the data collection in this way, multiple perspectives from various sources informed the ongoing data analysis of CoMPs in a holistic manner. As well as this, the overlapping phases helped to focus the interview data collection of phase three and inform the probes used within the participant logs from month to month.

Ethical considerations

As the study first and foremost dealt with people, various ethical procedures were engaged with. First, I had a dual researcher position within the research study

Table 2.1 Fieldwork plan and timeline overview

3 Phases	Research	Method	Timescale
Oct	Informal Meetings		
Nov	Doc/analysis	Video/Forums	P/Logs
Dec	Doc/analysis	Video/Forums	P/Logs
Jan	Doc/analysis	Video/Forums	P/Logs
Feb		Video/Forums	P/Logs
March		Video/Forums	P/Logs
April	Interviews	Video/Forums	P/Logs
May	Interviews	Video/Forums	P/Logs
June	Interviews		

where I was both researcher and lecturer in Limerick city, within the mid-west of Ireland. Often within the cases studied I had some contact with a few of the members of the music communities as well as the community 'gatekeepers' (such as leaders, policy makers, musical directors etc.) through professional and musical activities. Therefore, it was impossible to be totally detached from the situations being observed, and conclusions drawn must take this into account. Creswell asserts (2007b, p. 237), 'Our writing is an interpretation by us of events, people, and activities, and it is only our interpretation . . . our writing can only be seen as a discourse, one with tentative conclusions, and one that will be constantly changing and evolving'. I was therefore a *de facto* 'insider' (Creswell, 2007b, p. 44) or 'participant observer' (Cohen, Manion, & Morrison, 2007, pp. 310–14) in the study.

To ensure reflexivity, 'researcher effect' (Bogdan & Biklen, 2007) was taken into account throughout the design, collection and analysis of the data. Ethical procedures engaged in were:

- Choice of methods, such as the use of video and tripod to allow myself as researcher to partake in observation (and sit with the group as opposed to behind a camera) proved crucial for gaining trust and developing a relationship with the communities.
- 'Data triangulation' (Denzin & Lincoln, 2000) through large amounts of data from multiple sources collected helped ensure rigour and reliability in the findings.
- 'Theory triangulation' (Denzin & Lincoln, 2000) occurred throughout the research process, whereby multiple theories and perspectives were considered so that conclusions drawn were consistently reviewed.
- Trust and credibility in the researcher was aimed at through all participants in the study being made aware of the research purpose and questions through information sheets as well as informed consent forms. Participants were informed of the ongoing research and findings.
- Confidentiality and anonymity were maintained through the use of alias names for data analysis and write-up.

- Access with all participants and 'gatekeepers' was negotiated. Participants were made aware of their right to withdraw from the research process at any time.
- Member checks and respondent verification were carried out on interview transcripts and analysis write-ups to provide important feedback to the interpretive process. In this manner, the research sought to produce a 'recognisable reality' of the CoMP studied (Bryman & Burgess, 1994; Lincoln & Guba, 1985).

Further ethical considerations for the online case were required. Merriam states (2009, p. 162), 'explicitly considering and describing the impact of these factors is a new responsibility of the qualitative researcher'. The researcher role in examining the online community was one of a 'lurker'; essentially a participant-observer who does not input into online discussions. While there were concerns over the hidden nature of this role, gaining informed consent was of crucial importance here. Once permission was gained through the 'gatekeepers' (moderator and tutors), information about the research was posted on the discussion forum, Facebook page, monthly e-newsletter and an email was sent directly to all subscribers of the website. Participants were given assurances regarding the anonymity of their posts and were told they could withdraw from the research at any time or request that their posts on message boards would not be used.

Research methods

The collective case study gathered data through (a detailed breakdown of data gathered is provided in Appendix A):

- group data (video observations, focus group interviews);
- individual accounts (participant logs, individual interviews);
- online data (discussion forums, video tutorials, Facebook posts).

From a constructionist viewpoint, 'discourse' is manifest through meaningful musical and social practice within a community. Bourdieu, for example, continually emphasises the importance of language within his 'theory of practice' where exchanges in discourse are viewed as socially situated encounters (Bourdieu, 1977, 1984, 1990, 2002; Bourdieu & Johnson, 1993). Applying such a view to musical communities, joint musical interactions are seen as ways of making music together but also a means to 'interthink' through communicative processes (both verbal and non-verbal) (Littleton & Mercer, 2012; Mercer & Littleton, 2007). It is claimed (Mercer & Littleton, 2007, p. 4), 'people do not only interact, they "interthink", combining their intellects in creative ways that may achieve more than the sum of the parts'. Taking a sociocultural discourse analysis approach to investigate collective music-making, Littleton and Mercer (2012), emphasise talk and music as joint modes of communication. Musical and social practice can be viewed thus as intertwined within the study.

Video recording and observation

As the actions, behaviours, relationships and complex realities of CoMPs are at the centre of the inquiry, video recordings alongside observational field notes acted as the primary data collection methods for the two 'on the ground' cases of the jazz ensemble (LJW) and youth choir (CLYC). The video data was collected using a free-standing tripod so that the researcher could engage in observational field notes and also reflected the view that (Rahn, 2007, p. 303), 'In video research, it is more important to maintain an authentic relationship with the participant than it is to upstage that moment with stylized camera or editing work'. The video data and associated observation field notes gained first-hand information as it happened and so allowed for multiple viewings and 'freeze interactions . . . to capture behavioural nuances precisely' (Adler & Adler, 1994, p. 383). With multiple viewings, numerous opportunities for analysis and interpretation ensued where such things as patterns, critical incidents, relationships and roles could be observed. The dialogue from the workshop rehearsal session videos was transcribed verbatim and observational field notes taken during the sessions were added to the transcriptions. Through both observation and video data, both musical and social interactions could be analysed. MacDonald and Wilson argue (2005, p. 321), 'talking about music – as distinct from playing music – constitutes a considerable volume of their interaction time together as musicians . . . talk is seen as a tool of social action'.

Creswell advocates that unusual aspects of a situation or topics that participants may not be comfortable talking about generally can be discovered and understood through observation (Creswell, 2009, p. 179). There is a risk to reliability, however, as there is a large degree of 'interpretation' (Denscombe, 1999, p. 141) that occurs within observational research. The video recordings in addition to associated field notes then provided a distinct advantage in that they provided (Erickson, 2006, p. 177) 'a continuous and relatively comprehensive record of social interaction, a document that is to some extent phenomenologically neutral, that is the video recorder does not think while it records'. Thus, the video data helped to ensure as holistic an account as possible and reduced the threat of researcher bias while in the field. Using audio-visual tools, Gray and Mallins claim (2004, p. 95), 'The closer one can get to the medium of the original idea or experience the more likely it is to have impact and meaning'.

Steve Dillon in studying music community development programmes similarly employed the use of field notes alongside digital tools as he felt it allowed (2006, p. 273), 'the experience of arts making to remain in its symbolic form: music as music, and performance as performance, rather than solely as an abstract textual explanation'. The video recordings and associated field notes for Chapters 3 and 4 involved 10 two-hour rehearsals and two performances each over a period of seven months. Video data provided the best opportunity of capturing the practices that emerged during complex socio-musical interactions within these communities.

Interviews

The interviews employed in this study captured both individual and group perspectives from the CoMPs. Through the use of focus group and individual interviews, they can be classified as 'qualitative research interviews' (King, 1994, pp. 16–17) due to their focus on meaning, perceptions, human interactions and relationships. Robson states (Robson, 2002, p. 272), 'The human use of language is fascinating both as behaviour in its own right, and for the virtually unique window that it opens on what lies behind our actions'. All interviews took a 'semi-standardised approach' (Berg, 2007) to allow for predetermined questions/topic guides based on the research questions (outlined in the Introduction) while also admitting a degree of flexibility in the interview to such things as wording and order of questions. Appendix B outlines the interview schedules for participants within the CoMPs as well as the tutors/organisers. All interviews were carried out during the latter half of the nine-month fieldwork phase to allow for preliminary themes to be explored from the participant logs and video data as well as gaining trust within the communities over time for members to participate.

A focus group interview was deemed appropriate for participants in the jazz ensemble and youth choir. Here, group dynamics were capitalised on through a 'synergistic group effect' (Stewart & Shamdasani, 1990) where participants had the potential to 'spark off one another' (Rubin & Rubin, 1995, p. 140). However, a face-to-face individual interview was chosen as a more appropriate approach for the organisers and tutors to gain individual accounts, for their convenience and to ensure participation. Individual Skype interviews with the tutors of the online case (OAIM) were employed for the same reasons.

There are of course some limitations associated with interviewing often conceived as: a time-consuming process (Robson, 2002, p. 273), risks of receiving indirect information out of context (Creswell, 2009, p. 179), and reliability being under threat due to the impact of the interviewer, or 'interviewer effect' (Denscombe, 1999, p. 137). Despite this, the interview data complemented the other forms of data very well to expand understandings from individual insights into the development of CoMPs. The interviews carried out therefore provided further triangulation opportunities in the data gathered and analysed.

Participant logs

The data gathered from the participant logs intended to provide rich insights and understandings into members' perceptions of their experiences within CoMPs as they unfolded over time. This data form related directly to Wenger's (1998; 2002) focus on individuals' membership and roles within CoPs. Pitts employed such a method under the term 'diaries' across two of the four case studies in the larger musical participation research referred to previously (Pitts, 2005). This method gathered participant diaries from a music summer school and audience diaries from a Chamber Music Festival. Pitts remarks on the usefulness of the method (Pitts, 2005, p. 8), 'it proved to be invaluable for the insight they offered on the classes and interactions I had not observed, and the new perspectives on events I had witnessed but might have understood differently from the participants'.

Within this study of CoMPs, a selection of participants across the three cases maintained a log (or diary) of their participation within their musical community over a seven-month period. These logs were distributed, filled in and collected online using SurveyMonkey[1] following a discussion on what would suit their needs best (in the case of the online community, this was of course the obvious choice). The completion of the logs was voluntary and so while some members completed all logs, others were not as consistent. Therefore an average number was given in each case to approximate how many full logs were collected in total (see Appendix A). A decision was taken to include log entries in the data analysis as all of the data was deemed useful for providing individual insights into the study.

Four log entries were prompted over the nine months through a series of guiding questions (see Appendix C), with only subtle changes made between the three cases for relevance. The issues explored included: motivation, role, performance, creativity and types of learning encountered. The four entries were spread out over the fieldwork period to record individual reflections over time. Each log finished with a reflection opportunity for members to record a time when they really enjoyed being a part of their CoMP and a time when they did not enjoy being a part of their CoMP. Thus, the logs were semi-structured but with opportunities for self-directed discussion and reflection for the members. Guidelines and reminders were given verbally during observation sessions with each community and through email where applicable.

Online forums

To ensure reliability across the cases investigated, research methods employed for the online case attempted to be consistent in data gathering procedures as with the other two cases. In this manner, participant logs were posted online for participants to fill in and interviews occurred with the recognised leaders/tutors of the community. The use of text and discourse was especially relevant to the examination of the online community. In the same way that dialogue in the video observations of the LJW and CLYC played an important role in investigating their practices, collecting online dialogue through the OAIM discussion forums and Facebook posts was vital to building up a picture of this online CoMP as well.

Ewing, in his writings on cultures within online communities (2008, p. 584), advises, 'Immersion will allow a researcher to better understand the in-group and out-group dynamics that develop as a community culture evolves, and will help in interpretation'. Thus, without actually inputting directly, the activities and interactions of the members of the community were followed over a nine-month period. The CoP framework guided this data collection and analysis. Sections

---

1 SurveyMonkey (www.surveymonkey.com) is an online survey tool.

of the discussion forums and Facebook posts that proved most illuminating were saved, subsequently coded and analysed in the same manner as the other data gathered within and across cases. This approach to the online case as with the other two cases ensured this qualitative collective case study was 'anchored in real-life situations . . . and illuminates meanings that expand the reader's experiences' (Merriam, 2009, p. 51).

Analysing communities of musical practice

Due to the sociocultural theoretical perspectives and constructionist position underpinning this book (see Chapter 1), a thematic analysis shaped by such views was used in the data analysis. In particular, the CoP model was operationalised as an analytical tool during the cross-case comparison of the collective case study. This holistic analysis across all data sources served to illuminate relationships, themes and issues and related these to the larger theoretical framework and research questions of the study. The use of computer-assisted tools, in this instance the qualitative software package NVivo, was of significant benefit during this data analysis.

The analysis involved within-case analysis (Chapters 3, 4 and 5) and cross-case comparison (Chapter 6). The process was both inductive and deductive, allowing for emerging categories as well as a thematic analysis to occur. To strengthen the validity and reliability of the research, categories were refined, themes were established, meaningful patterns were detected, assumptions were tested and multiple perspectives were considered. Transcribed data from all cases was imported, given headings, labelled and organised within an NVivo project. The data gathered then went through four phases of analysis as described below:

- Phase one: This involved open coding the data as 'free' codes which was akin to an 'immersion approach' where the coding was mainly interpretive and fluid (Robson, 2002, p. 458). This open coding phase allowed for inductive themes to emerge through initial thoughts and reflections on the data gathered.
- Phase two: This entailed a 'template approach' (Robson, 2002, p. 458) to the original data analysis. The within-case analyses employed a thematic approach shaped by the sociocultural theoretical perspectives presented in Chapter 1. Key research themes of musical and community practices (see Chapters 3, 4 and 5) were used to categorise the data into broad themes, or 'tree codes'. The free codes from the first level of analysis were referred back to and assigned to one of the tree codes where relevant.
- Phase three: This phase sought out significant themes, incidents or actors within the data analysis. These significant findings were woven into the discussion of findings within the key themes of the within-case analyses. Memos, models and links were used in NVivo to add comments and reflections and to test out statements during this analysis. Text and word query searches aided this process too.

- Phase four: The cross-case comparison employed the three CoP dimensions of mutual engagement (domain), joint enterprise (community) and shared repertoire (practice) (Wenger, 1998, pp. 70–3). Conclusions were drawn from the three cases and then across cases. Within this holistic analysis, the 'constant comparative method' (Strauss & Corbin, 1998) was used where analysis of the data occurred while making comparisons, asking questions, drawing emergent categories and theories during data collection as well as post collection. The relationships, themes and issues were then combined and related to the larger theoretical framework of the research.

These phases of analysis drew on two particular music studies from Finnegan (2007) and Pitts (2005) where descriptions of each site/project or 'case' were followed by a thematic analysis and finally general reflections were drawn from the data analysis.

Summary

This chapter aimed to map out and justify the methodological rationale for the research undertaken. The paradigm of inquiry set out in Chapter 1 informed the methodological choices through a constructionist viewpoint which was further conceptualised among sociocultural theories. These lenses framed the research methodology and its analytical approaches. In investigating CoMPs, this worldview of focusing on the ways that distinct communities make meaning from and interpret their shared experiences and interactions shaped and underpinned the study. Thus, a qualitative collective case study was chosen to examine these CoMPs in-depth where a participant-observer researcher role was taken. The three cases selected were a purposive sample from the mid-west of Ireland with variations in genre, structures and age range, and one case was online. Fieldwork was carried out over a nine-month period where multiple qualitative methods comprised video recording, observations, interviews, participant logs and online forums. Through group and individual insights, these methods aimed to increase the depth and breadth of the data collection and analysis within the study.

Part II

Illustrations of communities of musical practice

3 A jazz community

Eric:	Brian can't make it for a very un-rock 'n' roll reason.
Jimmy:	He got a job?
Eric:	No, that would be a jazz reason.
Jimmy:	Yeah.
Eric:	No, this is just un-rock 'n' roll. He has to mind his granny tonight.

(LJWV2[1])

Every community of musical practice (CoMP) exists within certain local, national and international contexts. Each one has particular norms, rules, structures, interactions and 'practices' distinct to their collective situations. The short exchange above taken from a jazz ensemble rehearsal reveals much about group music-making from the penchant for insider jokes, to values and beliefs about musical identity. Examining a jazz community provides an in-depth understanding of the links between individuals and communities as they are mediated through music-making.

As a first illustration of a CoMP, the Limerick Jazz Workshop (LJW) is an adult ensemble-based teaching and performing initiative based in Limerick city, in the mid-west region of Ireland (see Chapter 1 for contextual details). The group studied comprised five male instrumentalists (on saxophone, bass guitar, vibraphone, drums and flute) and two female singers, with two more male instrumentalists (on guitars) joining halfway through the research period. This research focused specifically on the 'advanced' jazz ensemble, as chosen by the LJW coordinator out of four possible ensembles. LJW sessions lasted two hours and took place on Tuesday evenings. The workshops ran in autumn and spring semesters of 12 weeks each and after about six weeks the ensembles had a performance in local venues. There was no restriction on the age range and the ensemble studied varied in age from early 20s to mid-50s. Two of the members held dual roles alongside being participants in the ensemble. Jimmy, the bass guitarist, was the tutor and Eric, the saxophone player, was also the overall LJW coordinator. The members had all been with the ensemble over a period of two to five years. Four

---

1 LJWV2 refers to Limerick Jazz Workshop Video 2. All video data is classified in this way, with the number indicating the sequence of the video recording session.

nationalities were represented in the ensemble: Irish, German, Italian and English. The repertoire chosen (by the tutor and members) was from a broad jazz style and ranged from jazz 'standards' to contemporary jazz to jazz fusion pieces. This ensemble, as the most advanced of the LJW (as determined through auditions), often performed at city events and festivals.

The group's practices, seen as 'things we do and develop' (Burnard, 2012b, p. 266), are delineated here by a discussion of community and musical practices. Following this, the distinctive practice of creativity, which was particularly unique to the LJW, is presented. Drawing on observations, video data, interviews and participant logs that were collected over nine months, the ensemble's community, musical and distinctive creativity practices map out the *modus operandi* of this CoMP.

Community practices

The jazz ensemble acquired, shared, negotiated and situated knowledge through community practices to 'transform' their world (Wenger, 1998). From a socio-cultural viewpoint, learning for the ensemble happened to a large degree through community practices of 'collaborative knowledge building' (Scardamalia & Bereiter, 1991, 1996). Thus, practices emerged through group interaction and participation within the ensemble both in rehearsal sessions and performances.

Group perspectives

The LJW rehearsal sessions without exception always started late (by approximately 20 minutes). Members joined the group in a casual relaxed manner often not greeting each other verbally but simply acknowledging entry into the room with a nod or eye contact. Frequently, neither a verbal nor non-verbal greeting was imparted but members simply picked up their instruments and began practising some small motif or line that would later be performed; almost like a warm-up exercise. All of this was done with an overriding sense of the familiar, as if there was no need for 'hellos' and this informal atmosphere was maintained throughout the sessions.

From observing and recording interactions some norms and routines of a rehearsal session emerged. Jimmy and Eric were always on time (they held the dual roles of playing in the ensemble and also as tutor and LJW coordinator respectively). This often gave the two members the opportunity to casually chat while waiting for the rest of the ensemble to arrive. The interconnectedness of musical and social interactions was apparent here where Jimmy and Eric practised small sections of music as a type of warm-up between chatting. A further norm saw Jimmy typically inviting participation with a casual question such as, 'Do you want to try that?', taking up a leadership role to initiate group playing.

The dialogical interactions within the ensemble predominantly centred on jazz music, stemming from a jazz canon and to an even greater extent jokes or anecdotes about jazz. The use of 'jazz lore' – essentially jazz stories, anecdotes and jokes typically referencing 'jazz legends' – was genre-specific and so facilitated inculcation into values, concepts and traditions of jazz music. Jazz lore was revealed to be a regular aspect of the rehearsal practices, signifying a distinctive community discourse between members of the ensemble. Furthermore, a community practice of shared group responsibility for choosing the ensemble's repertoire was also apparent throughout rehearsals, where books, CDs and scores were often exchanged between players to source new repertoire.

Two 'newcomers' joined the ensemble halfway during the research period. Ryan on acoustic guitar and Ken on electric guitar expanded the group to nine. These members were subsumed into the ensemble in a casual manner and it emerged informally that Ryan was an old member returning to the LJW and Ken was a good friend of Jimmy's. Despite this change in membership, the community practices of the ensemble remained intact to a large degree. For instance, the rehearsal sessions still started and finished late, a casual atmosphere was retained and jazz lore continued to be employed. Likewise, the musical practices involved the same non-verbal cues and behaviours regular to jazz jamming sessions that were evident previous to the change. Thus, this relationship-building through music-making and participation, where music is part of the social life of this group, relates strongly to the writings of Pitts (2005) and Turino (2008) explored in previous chapters.

While the community practices stayed largely unaffected by the group change, the relationships within the group shifted, having an impact on the group dynamic. For example, the exchange of jazz lore between Jimmy and Eric that was so prevalent now also included Ryan who similarly enjoyed sharing jazz anecdotes, jokes and stories:

Jimmy: Did you bring your sax on your skiing holiday?
Eric: Nope!
Jimmy: . . . there's your problem
Ryan: He'd be out on the slopes with it – with his saxophone, fingers frozen . . .
Jimmy: Absolutely. Can't imagine Coltrane on skis (all chuckle)
Eric: Ray Brown played a little golf . . .
Ryan: . . . yeah out walking the whole time (clicks a few times) and swinging
Jimmy: You know that story, Ella Fitzgerald and Ray Brown creep on stage before a gig and he emptied a bag of marbles into the piano so when eh Oscar Peterson, when he started playing piano, marbles started to shoot out of the piano (laughter)

(LJWV6)

This extract demonstrated how seamlessly the members dropped in lore about jazz musicians even though there was not necessarily a specific connection. Here, jazz 'masters' were brought into the conversation through a reference to a personal skiing holiday, Ray Brown was mentioned as having played golf and this led onto a story about Ella Fitzgerald and a bag of marbles! All of this was done in a jovial manner but created a community for such domain-specific dialogue (clearly due to the existence of a jazz canon) to take place, acting as a source of common interest between members. This laidback atmosphere was also an important means of enculturation into the values of jazz music and its form of group music-making. Furthermore, through this interactive process of building 'musical common knowledge' (Miell & Littleton, 2008) a collective musical identity was formed.

The individual musical identities of the ensemble members were joked at too in this extract, where it was imagined in a good-humoured way that Eric was so committed to his saxophone that he might bring it with him on a skiing holiday. Jimmy, Eric and Ryan engaged in this style of discourse very often throughout the video analysis and others appeared to enjoy the exchanges too. This 'fun' element within the community often functioned as a way to lighten the mood, as a tool for learning, to promote a feeling of belonging or simply as a break from the intensity of playing (Chapter 6 provides a more detailed discussion on the function of 'fun' within a CoMP).

The singers joined the instrumental players halfway through a rehearsal at roughly 8pm. Up until this the singers attended a specialist singing ensemble class. A break then ensued where the talk was casual, friendly and predominantly centred again on jazz lore or exchanging information regarding gigs and recordings. The breaks in the rehearsal sessions demonstrated various aspects of community practices where social interaction was a significant part of their group identity. It was clear that while there was a strong sense of inclusion within the community through a shared sense of fun, laughter and talk that included personal information (such as holidays, work etc.), there was evidence of exclusion too. For example, at one break, it emerged that a past member had caused 'trouble' previously and the ensemble did not want them to return. There were hints that this related to unwanted egotism during their time within the ensemble which the members did not see as fitting with the group's identity. This was reminiscent of the 'toxic coziness' (Wenger, 1998) and 'in-group/out-group' status (Turino, 2008) that can occur within communities discussed in Chapter 1.

There were diverse and overlapping memberships within the ensemble also, which Moran and John-Steiner (2004, p. 12) argue is a key characteristic to gaining 'complementarity' in collaborations. Diversities of gender, musical background, race, roles of instrumentalist/singer as well as professional/amateur were all-important here. The most obvious example of this was in the two distinct memberships of the instrumentalists who were all male and singers who were all female. Whether or not such a distinction was made due to gender, or the delineation of singers and instrumentalists, or the fact that the singers joined the ensemble halfway through a workshop session remains a complex issue. It was perhaps a result of all of these factors. What was wholly apparent, however, was the change in dynamics, relationships and forms of musical communication as well as teaching and learning approaches when the singers entered rehearsal sessions and performances.

By way of illustration, the excerpt below follows on from a period of 15 minutes where Leona was working as a solo-singer with the ensemble on 'Born to be Blue'. Previous to the dialogue below and following Jimmy's advice to experiment to a greater degree, Leona had been re-singing sections continually. While open to this approach, Leona was visibly emotionally tired from the critique. At this point, the other members of the group began to lighten the mood and provide mutual support as seen in the dialogue below:

Jimmy: I don't think you are being challenged at all doing it that way. It sounds very comfortable for you to do it.

Eric: And that wouldn't do at all (laughs)

Jack: (laughing) Come on, we are all under pressure here (waving his vibes beater at Leona) you've gotta be under pressure with us.

Leona: A few sleepless nights ahead so (laughs)

(LJWV2)

The sense of camaraderie exemplified here pervaded throughout rehearsal and performance sessions. Joint membership was reassured through Jack's comment, 'you've gotta be under pressure with us', illustrating a togetherness with the singers that sometimes was not as obvious as it was between the instrumentalists. This projected a sentiment of 'we are in this together' which, coupled with shared laughter, aided a sense of community among the group and in the above instance acted as an immediate reassurance to the singer.

In addition, the instrumentalists often took on encouraging or supportive roles towards the singers – more than what they would normally show each other as seen above (they also helped the singers set up the microphone equipment during rehearsals). While the session remained relaxed and casual there was also a shift in Jimmy's tutoring style to a more didactic role than seen in the previous half of the sessions, such as encouraging the singers to 'try', emphasising experimentation and detailing how to approach this: 'try to improvise on the words'. The singers too adopted more traditional student/teacher roles than the instrumentalists did with Jimmy, such as seeking instruction and praise, and looking more explicitly for musical cues and gestures.

Within the community practices of the ensemble, there was a sense of induction into a 'world of jazz' or jazz canon involving all of its values, stories, traditions, jokes and jargon. Jimmy as the band leader/tutor of the jazz ensemble and therefore 'expert' took on the role of inducting the other members, echoing Wenger's arguments on apprenticeship learning (1998) discussed in Chapter 1. As part of this role, he imparted jazz lore frequently during the rehearsal sessions and often as a learning tool in itself:

Jimmy: . . . that's why Miles Davis was such a great guy because he just didn't give a shit, like he just did exactly what he wanted whenever he wanted and you got all the different phases in his career then. You got so much different music out there. I mean he could have just played those ballads that he did in the 50s until he died . . . you know someone said to him once; why don't you play that stuff anymore? He said 'I thought we got it right the first time'.

(LJWV9)

In this extract, we see clearly an admiration being passed on from Jimmy for Miles Davis who was 'a great guy' who did not give in to 'popular' demands. Here Jimmy used a jazz 'legend' to try and challenge the members to be more experimental and creative in their approaches to playing jazz music. The quip from Miles Davis, 'I thought we got it right the first time', is humorous but also functions as a tool for learning about the culture of jazz and tradition of challenging playing.

Jimmy was absent in one of the 10 rehearsal sessions studied which proved to be illuminating in examining leadership within the ensemble outside of an explicit tutoring role. Here a teaching substitute was brought in from another ensemble within the LJW but rather than this person taking the reins, Jack, the vibraphone player within the group, assumed the leadership role. This rehearsal session exemplified a form of 'context-dependent alternating leadership' often found in ensemble practices (Murphy McCaleb, 2014). From the video data, it was obvious that Jack was taking the position of 'expert' in the ensemble – directing the music, instructing players' entries, guiding the substitute and making the decision on when the session finished. This was not altogether surprising with Jack being the only other professional musician aside from Jimmy within the ensemble, and in other rehearsals he often sought a co-leadership role alongside Jimmy.

However, Jimmy's absence also encouraged other members to become involved to a greater degree. There was much more shared responsibility and joint decision-making evident (despite Jack's assumption of leadership), as revealed in this extract where a substitute for Jimmy plays with the group:

> *Jack makes a vocal drum noise to indicate the tempo*
> *Eric*:   Not all of it is that quick
> *Ken*:   No it's . . .
> *Eric*:   . . . Some of it's at half time
> *Jack*:   . . . half time for ye, half time for you (to Brian) but it's fast like
>   *Jack hits his beaters again to set the tempo. Brian copies and*
>   *plays along on drums. The substitute enters on guitar*
> *Jack*:   I don't know how fast we can do it, you want to try it?
> *Substitute*: Yeah
> *Jack*:   Okay (hits sticks) a one two, a one two three four . . .
>   *All play*
> *Jack*:   Okay (looks at Eric, laughs, sings the tune and drum beat, then
>   sings again to sub) it's arranged like that. Okay, one, two (hits
>   sticks for tempo, slower this time) one, two, three, four.
>
>   (LJWV8)

While Jack remained very much 'in charge' here, there is a more shared sense of responsibility between Eric and Jack. Brian and Ken, however, remained peripheral to any decision-making; content, it appeared, to take instruction. The substitute during this exchange stayed at the margins due to the group already having a shared practice established. Aware of this, he waited to be 'invited in' by the 'oldtimers' (Wenger, 1998) or established members of the group where we see Jack asking, 'you want to try it?' in the same leadership manner seen previously with Jimmy.

Just as the rehearsal sessions never began on time, they also never finished on time. The ending of a session was dictated not by the clock but by the music. If more pieces had to be played through or the group were intently working on one piece, they would simply keep going. As with the start of each session, this was done in a laidback manner but with the purpose of continuing the hard work of rehearsal. Often the session would go on until 9.30pm and sometimes up until 10pm (usually the last session before a performance). No one ever announced it was finished; rather, there was a shared implicit understanding that once both vocalists had sung through their pieces and were happy, the session was over. In this way the workshops almost always ended in a non-verbal manner through gestures of people packing up their instruments, talking to each other (and the researcher) and walking to their cars.

Distinctive community performance practices or jazz performance traditions were evident within the two public performances analysed. For example, during each solo/duet/trio section, non-verbal gestures were employed where the members of the ensemble not playing bowed their heads and appeared to listen attentively. The singers stood aside or crouched down to allow the instrumental soloists the limelight for that period. The improvisations appeared very free and almost seamlessly the players took up their sections. Non-verbal gestures were often used here where a player would glance at Jimmy who gave a nod when it was their turn or Jimmy touched his head to indicate to go back to the main tune ('the head'), as is common in a jazz session.

At the two performances, not all of the musicians took the same positions as in rehearsal. Jimmy in both gigs took a place in the background which indicated strongly the tutor's desire to hand over responsibility to the group, as was also evident in rehearsal. In the tradition of jazz the singers took centre stage. Jimmy did assume a leadership role evidenced in him introducing each tune during the performance, giving details of who composed the piece or was famous for performing it. As well as this, jokes were included in the performances through Jimmy over the microphone, often in a banter-like style as was common at rehearsals. For instance, Jimmy introduced the band in a very tongue-in-cheek manner with personal anecdotes for each member. For example, he introduced Jack as 'Limerick's premier and only vibes player – the best and the worst'. The ensemble was amused by all of this and appeared to enjoy the attention given to each introduction.

Through the analysis of both rehearsal sessions and performances, group perspectives of community practices revealed jazz lore, collaboration, non-verbal behaviours, genre-specific norms as well as distinct roles and relationships specific to this CoMP. These were corroborated through individual perspectives on community practices.

Individual perspectives

The members of the ensemble joined and stayed in the ensemble for reasons that were both musical and social. They wanted to learn, be challenged and make music as a collective, as they related in interview:

> I've done loads of kind of courses and training and all of that and I realised that I had to really practise playing with other people and singing with other people . . . I thought it would be a great way to actually learn how to play with a band.
>
> (Leona)

> wanted the opportunity to play with other musicians and just to have that kind of live contact and I suppose in terms of for me it was a learning curve, it generates a very real and a positive pressure that you have to learn the stuff because you can be doing it at home and you can let stuff slide, so it's a good discipline.
>
> (Ryan)

Within the participant logs too, the opportunity to play with other musicians, participate and communally share music with people of similar interests arose as a significant motivation to join and indeed stay within the LJW. One member commented that when they joined, 'it was just good to be with similar-minded people and play music together' (Beatrice). This resonated with the LJW coordinator's motivation to set up the LJW, 'I founded LJW so as to create an opportunity to play jazz with like-minded people in Limerick' (Eric).

As the participants of the ensemble had all been members for over two to five years, the changes in perceived roles and membership over time were noted in the logs. Terms such as 'improving', 'developing', 'more confident' and 'experienced' were used frequently to describe this perceived progression. Some members noted this development through musical contributions but in equal measure individuals noted social interactions as having developed or changed for them within the group over time:

> I started as the drummer and moved to vibes making my role more harmonic/ melodic than rhythmic.
>
> (Jack)

> Playing is on balance improving – that means I can make more of a contribution musically.
>
> (Ryan)

> I am also much more friendly with the rest of the band, and feel more as an equal to them now: when I started, I felt more like the intruder!
>
> (Leona)

I was very shy and held back in what I started singing and performing . . . I am more confident now.

(Beatrice)

As revealed in the above extracts, defining roles, musical contributions and social interactions all indicated individual accounts of community practices. Longevity of membership was important here for inclusion, especially for the female singers of the group. The male members of the ensemble defined their membership within the group as mainly musical as opposed to the females who related a more inter-related sense of their musical and social interactions. These differences could be related to gender but could also be a result of the delineated musical roles (singers/ instrumentalists) within the community. The fact that the singers joined the group halfway through the rehearsal sessions may also explain the initial perceived struggle for inclusion when they first joined the ensemble.

Jimmy at interview commented on the change of dynamic within the group when the singers joined at rehearsal. He saw this as nothing to do with gender or jazz music but attributed it to the singers often not being as musically competent as the instrumentalists, as well as culturally embedded musical roles that saw the singers gaining more public and monetary recognition than instrumentalists, stating:

it's almost like you know the star is the singer and there's probably cultural resentment among musicians over the years, it's probably embedded environmentally you know that this bastard is going to get more money than us, gonna get more everything than us . . . you'll even see it in local pub bands you know.

(Jimmy)

Furthermore, there was a diversity of membership due to the musical backgrounds which people brought to the ensemble. Members were aware of this distinction and Ryan noted:

I wouldn't describe myself as a jazz musician but I would see myself as you know trying to be within, trying to have a place within that broader tradition and trying to understand the music, appreciate the music and be very conscious. I certainly wouldn't in anyway be putting myself in that category of professional players but have that sense of being a very small part of that broader tradition.

Here Ryan recognised his limits but still felt there was a place for him to be 'a small part' of the jazz 'tradition' through being a member of this community.

Roles and identity formation within the ensemble were defined through community practices of varying types of membership and this was also evident through leadership. It was clear that Jimmy, the ensemble tutor, was seen as the 'expert' to lead the ensemble and he was paid for such knowledge. Ryan articulated the practice of this community as being passed on through such leadership, also mentioning Jack's co-leadership role evidenced previously:

> I would see kind of music as a folk tradition where there's a core legacy and a canon which passes from generation to generation and I think if you read and even talk to some of the musicians, you know talk to Jack or Jimmy that idea of there is a tradition and they are passing on learning on site . . . then periodically it refreshes itself and goes off in terms of a new direction.

As well as learning from 'experts', the learning was also seen to occur through community practices of participation and membership in the 'art world' (Becker, 2008). Ryan also pointed to the social process of this learning where the rules and focus were consistently in negotiation, and shaped through its members. Ultimately, then, the practices and performance were a result of 'a network of cooperating people, all of whose work is essential to the final outcome' (Becker, 2008, p. 25).

Despite this leadership role, Jimmy encouraged collective group responsibility to a large degree. At interview, Jimmy related how pleased he was when such a collaborative learning approach paid off in performance:

> the performance of that song with Beatrice, Enda and Ryan, just the three of them went fantastic I thought because now they have a bit of confidence to even look at each other you know and just nod . . . simple things like that . . . that was great I think because there were no teachers involved, the three of them were there on their own.

This also pointed to the members accumulating knowledge over time, developing confidence as Jimmy pointed out and essentially embodying the shared community practices of the group indicated through such tools as non-verbal gestures during playing.

This sense of group responsibility was present throughout the analysis of the jazz ensemble. Absenteeism and not feeling up to standard musically was referred to with guilt as seen in Leona's comment, 'I missed a lot of sessions due to work, and I felt very bad about it – letting the band down' and Eric reinforced this, 'some of the tunes we are doing are a huge stretch for my technique and I don't like to let down the other group members'.

All interviews revealed that the ensemble developed practices at both musical and community levels due to the impact of the continuity of membership within the group that in turn had a positive impact on the music-making itself and a sense of community. The community practices of a shared, collective and challenging approach to learning were shaped by a community with shared interests, making 'friends' with the other members and continued participation in the ensemble.

The jazz ensemble acquired, shared, negotiated and situated community practices through their interactions and participation within the group. The community practices of the jazz ensemble can be characterised then as the overarching practices of: a prevailing casual atmosphere, interplay between leadership and group responsibility, integration of musical and social interactions, use of jazz lore and defined identities through varying memberships.

Musical practices

Collective music-making in the jazz genre formed the basis for this CoMP. Musical practices developed within the ensemble through sustained relationships built up over time. Small relates, 'the act of musicking establishes in the place where it is happening a set of relationships, and it is in those relationships that the meaning of the act lies' (1998, p. 13). Building relationships through musical practices was found to be a key theme within this jazz ensemble which had echoes with other jazz ensemble studies (Berliner, 1994; MacDonald & Wilson, 2005; Sawyer, 2003; Seddon & Biasutti, 2009; Seddon, 2005).

Group perspectives

Starting actual music-making occurred in a relaxed habitual manner, both in rehearsals and performances, with the members unhurried to begin as discussed earlier. Jimmy, as tutor, always took the first step to initiate group playing, inviting the other members of the ensemble to take part. This instruction was always carried out in a collaborative, equable way as opposed to any authoritarian or top-down style of tutoring. The first half of the rehearsal sessions continued in this manner between the musicians with short lead-ins to pieces. There was no prior discussion on what would be played or how; rather the tunes simply began and issues were dealt with between or after playing.

Tunes were played and continually reflected on for improvement, with Jimmy often taking a leadership role in this. He led the players' musical practices, tackling pieces of music in new, experimental and creative ways as seen in the following example:

Jimmy: So maybe this time just completely make it looser, make it much more open . . . Just when we got to yours Eric you know kind of be-boppy places, maybe do something funkier or something . . . just have a think about the way you played and see if you just try something that's almost alien to the way you normally approach it. So that you're pushing yourself into just a different territory, because otherwise it's gonna be always the same way. So I'll tell you what – we'll do three short improvs em eh (puts hand to head and points in turn to Enda, Eric and Jack) okay so you've got the mixolydian, super-locrian, phrygian – F D F and we'll do a very short one and maybe go round a few times if we can loop it around and try and each time we'll follow you okay?

(LJWV1)

Here Jimmy guided the ensemble in creative approaches to playing through suggestion as well as technical guides, such as jazz modes (phrygian and so on). He often spoke in motivational tones at length on these occasions (10 minutes of talk from Jimmy was common throughout the video data transcriptions), speaking here of doing something 'different', 'alien', 'pushing' oneself and moving into 'different territory'. Jimmy was very much in 'expert' or leader mode here, facilitating the other members of the ensemble to play in new, creative ways.

The group typically responded well to this type of encouragement. For instance, in playing the tune 'Thousand Island Park' within one rehearsal session, the solo improvisational sections demonstrated the effect advice from Jimmy had on the group. The collaborative nature of playing together was also highlighted. Jack and Brian's improvisation on vibes and drums stood out as being particularly experimental. Here Jack picked up the mood set by Enda initially in his flute solo. In this manner, Jack played long, sustained notes and Brian provided sparse percussive sounds on drums. While Brian began by looking to Jimmy at the beginning of the vibes solo, after about a minute, his sole attention turned to Jack and the two of them appeared immersed in an improvised duet between vibes and drums. Once these solos finished, Jimmy did not respond to the changes in playing and the experimental, creative nature applied to them but rather invited the members to try playing in further new ways. This lack of praise for the instrumentalists and stress on experimentation through creative playing was a consistent feature of the ensemble.

Jazz lore and recordings were used by Jimmy and the group members as learning tools to make connections to jazz techniques and styles. Jimmy employed this jazz lore as a significant mechanism to impart and mediate learning about such musical elements of style, technique and structure but also just as significantly about the principles and values of jazz music. Such lore was essentially 'negotiated' collectively to make meaning relevant to their situation and collective musical practices. It also acted as a symbol of musical identity in their jazz world and so formed a common ground for their relationships with each other.

Learning music from notation (or tablature in the case of the guitarists) as well as learning by ear was promoted. At rehearsal sessions, Jimmy also used the CD player as a group learning tool to play along to as well as listen out for stylistic and structural changes in tunes. Learning from recordings was repeatedly seen as important to learning jazz throughout the sessions. The pedagogy and learning routines of the group reveal the characteristic step-by-step approach taken by the ensemble led by Jimmy to learn new repertoire:

Jimmy: . . . so we might just have a look at this (gets CDs from his bag and passes them out) . . . for some reason the last bar didn't come out so the last six notes are missing but if you get that far I'm sure you can manage the last six (Jack laughs).

Some members try a few notes on their instruments. All looking intently at the sheet music and nod at Jimmy from time to time while he is talking.

Jimmy:	It's handy enough you know, it's just rhythmically, it's a little bit tricky but it's just all in D minor so I had to fiddle with it. So Ryan, myself and Ken have a separate bass part . . . that was on the direction that Leona gave me . . . maybe if we just try eh Ryan and Ken – you've got a part there where you got either two notes in a bar or four notes in a bar so two notes or two beats each and the four notes or one beat each okay? So can we just try our part first? All right so we'll just do it really slowly for a minute – I haven't played this myself . . .
Ken:	We'll keep it slow for you Jimmy (everyone laughs)

(LJWV6)

Jimmy assumed a dominant leadership role to guide the new learning; however, all of this was done in a laidback manner; he invited other members to take part, 'maybe we'll try first . . .'. The group responded well to this and all appeared very comfortable with this mode of learning. Jimmy's leadership and expertise was further asserted in the group through a joke in the extract where all members laugh at the idea of him having to slow down a tune to learn it, 'We'll keep it slow for you Jimmy'. In an expert/apprentice style of learning there was a focus on a lot of repetition of musical phrases and riffs following this exchange, with Jimmy calling out bars and keeping the pulse as well as standard notation being used. In this way, it mirrored a very formal and traditional method of music teaching.

Equally, there were informal teaching and learning methods present. Not all of the members read standard notation; in these cases, other forms (such as tablature) were provided or the player learned by ear. Despite the obvious nature of Jimmy 'teaching' a tune to the group in the previous extract, there were many signs of shared learning throughout the learning of a tune. For instance, it is noted that Leona as singer on this tune has given some direction for the instrumentalists; furthermore, at one point in learning the above tune Jack hit the right note repeatedly to reinforce it after Eric had played the wrong one. This was carried out in a very fluid, spontaneous, non-verbal manner. Over the 10 rehearsal sessions observed, as the group became more confident with a tune they began to: refer to each other more often, run through small passages individually or in twos or threes during small gaps of time in the workshop, play less from notation, engage in far more non-verbal cues during playing, and generally become much more creative with their playing.

Recordings of jazz music emerged as important learning tools and influences on the ensemble's musical practices. These tools within the group linked directly to the certain reverence so often given to the jazz masters in jazz lore explored earlier. There was evidence of 'collaborative knowledge building' (Scardamalia & Bereiter, 1991, 1996) here through relationships with regard to recordings; frequently members recommended certain albums, artists or YouTube links to each other. This resonated deeply with Sawyer's research into jazz groups where he found that listening to the jazz greats, leading figures and jazz albums was hugely important in providing knowledge in the domain for subsequent collective music-making (2003, p. 52).

In the two performances observed the jazz ensemble took to the stage once the previous ensemble were finished. The players then spent roughly five minutes in much the same manner as they would in a rehearsal session, playing their instruments individually, going over small riffs etc. The atmosphere, although casual, was not as relaxed among the players as during rehearsals seen in a stiffening of body gestures, repeated warming-up exercises on instruments and much double-checking of instructions with each other.

Within each performance the ensemble entered into long improvisatory sections, lasting anywhere between 10 and 15 minutes. These sections were where the group appeared to most enjoy themselves and equally the sections that the audience appreciated the most with much clapping and encouraging call-outs occurring as the players became more experimental. The group responded to this well and rose to the expectations of the audience to keep up challenging playing and singing. Towards the end of both gigs, a few very capable individual players from other ensembles were invited up by Jimmy to play with the ensemble and a typical instrumental jazz jam session ensued. In both gigs observed the ensemble played for over an hour. All of this was done with great fluidity as opposed to the interrupted nature of a rehearsal and so encouraged 'flow' (Csikszentmihalyi, 1996) within the performance.

The professional status of two of the players, Jack and Jimmy, differentiated musical practices within the ensemble's performances. These co-leadership roles were very apparent where Jack and Jimmy led the group through assigning a sequence of solos, giving musical cues, setting the tempo and starting and ending the tune. Within one particular musical performance Jack and Jimmy acted as co-leaders, verbally and non-verbally assigning solo sequences to the ensemble as the singers duetted unaccompanied. They also reasserted the tempo during the singers' improvisation and the other members looked over to gain this instruction non-verbally. There appeared to be a lack of trust in the singers keeping the tempo here which may have been a gender issue or a singer/instrumentalist way of working. A whole-group improvisation with a return to the head of the tune every so often was guided by either Jack or Jimmy through non-verbal gestures such as nods or Jack hitting the first few notes of the main tune very loudly for the others to follow suit.

The improvisatory sections of performance highlighted the process of collective music-making developing into a shared performance practice. According to Bourdieu, knowledge is gained through social practice or 'ways of doing' within 'fields of practice'. He identifies field positioning of key players, power relations, dispositions, networks and resources as some of the factors involved in playing the 'game of culture' (Bourdieu, 1977, 1984, 1990, 2002). Jazz improvisations also contain a certain 'etiquette' (Becker, 2008; Berliner, 1994; Sawyer, 2002, 2003, 2006). This jazz ensemble relied largely on what Seddon and Biasutti (2009) describe as 'musical communication' for the group to explicitly and implicitly learn and negotiate the 'rules of the game' (Bourdieu, 1984) of improvisatory performance. This learning occurred in a collaborative participatory way through relationships, which was seen in the playing of tunes onstage. Here through language and gesture it was obvious that improvisations were being negotiated 'in the moment'. Jack and Jimmy took on the leadership roles, being the most experienced/professional players, and the other members looked to them for direction during the performances. All of this was carried out in a familiar manner although certain 'rules' were abided by such as how many bars to play for, when to return to the tune and keeping the tempo.

Throughout the analysis the shared musical practices of advancing the playing of jazz music, learning within a collective, building confidence to play in new ways and performing in live situations were evident from the group perspectives gathered.

Individual perspectives

Performance itself was seen as highly important to all members and a way of gauging progression. Log entries referred to the end product of performance as being an important driver to the process of rehearsing:

> It's an opportunity to gauge how well my playing is coming on.
>
> (Ryan)

> Ultimate goal is performance . . . seeing all the hard work and practice come to fruition.
>
> (Jack)

> it's what drives you to practice.
>
> (Ken)

From these quotes, we see a direct link members made between the musical practices of rehearsing and performance. It was viewed as the 'ultimate goal' or final outcome of the rehearsal process. Performance was seen as an opportunity to evaluate progression in playing but also as pivotal to the enjoyment of being part of the ensemble and in doing so defined the relationships within the ensemble. Jimmy communicated that one of the great successes of the LJW were the live performances which he claimed were:

> bridging the gap from playing in front of your family or sitting in your own house and going up on stage – because you know you're there for the taking when you're on stage and there's always a clown in the corner who'll say something to you . . . it takes a huge amount of courage but then it breeds more self-confidence.
>
> (Jimmy)

Practice routines revealed a strong commitment to the ensemble's progression as musical performers. Time spent on practising material for the LJW ranged from one to five hours per week. These musical practices were revealed as being quite different between the instrumentalists and singers, echoing similar group differences discussed earlier. The instrumentalist practice routines focused on technique and skills whereas the singers relied much more on recordings as well as e-learning tools, such as YouTube. In addition, both singers mentioned the influence of the LJW tutor's advice in guiding their practice, whereas the instrumentalists did not. This resonated with the shift in Jimmy's tutoring style evident as being more instructive with the singers than the instrumentalists and so the singers in response cast themselves in more traditional student/teacher roles than the instrumentalists.

Each member noted the need to practise due to the high challenge of the LJW and also a sense of responsibility to the rest of the group. Leona related, 'the musicians are all extremely good and I want to be prepared adequately to fit in with them'. Ryan also claimed that playing with an ensemble influenced his practising, 'to think about the totality of playing – my sound and feel; strengths and weaknesses; discipline of playing with other musicians; areas that I need to work on in terms of theory and technical aspects of playing'. There was an overriding sense here of group responsibility and accountability among the members as regards playing as an ensemble.

Eric's founding expectations for the LJW were to have public performances and increase what he referred to as 'risk-taking' in playing. Playing within a group where there was a challenge and progression in learning was what motivated many of the ensemble members to join initially but also to sustain their membership. Eric claimed, 'all these guys are much, much better than me (laughs) but it's better for me to be getting sort of musically beaten up'. Jimmy expressed his opinion on pushing people out of their 'comfort zone' as strongly as he facilitated this in practice, stating 'I really don't see the point of people coming playing stuff that they're absolutely comfortable with . . . even if they learn one or two new things it breeds certain confidences . . . the confidence thing is a huge factor in it because if you're anyway lacking in confidence it really affects the way you play'. Jimmy consistently encouraged creativity through improvisation and so commented on the need to challenge the players, learn new ways of playing music and so build confidence through the ensemble.

The link with the Limerick Jazz Society gigs (referred to in Chapter 1) was also mentioned as part of their musical practices, musical influences and added social dimension of the jazz workshop:

> before I joined this I didn't go to as many jazz gigs because not that many of my friends are into jazz and sometimes I just didn't want to be alone because I didn't know anybody . . . and now because I know enough people from here I know that even if I show up at Dolans by myself I know that there's going to be someone there and it's a way to get to see really good gigs . . . and learn from them too.
>
> (Leona)

These intersecting communities of the Limerick Jazz Society and Limerick Jazz Workshop were also seen by both Jimmy and Eric as all-important to the holistic musical development of the members' musical practices. Live performance was viewed as critical in this progression, just as recordings were frequently used as learning tools.

The jazz ensembles' musical practices were characterised through sustained relationships built up over time seen through such practices as the use of jazz lore as an enculturation and learning tool, to non-verbal gestures such as nodding and eye contact. Both formal and informal pedagogies where both leadership and collaborative learning approaches were promoted both within rehearsals and performances defined this ensemble's identity to a large degree. The practice of learning through live performance was also reinforced as essential to the ensemble's musical practices and means of building confidence in playing.

Distinctive practice: creativity

Creativity emerged as a distinctive practice within this community. 'Creativity' within this book is conceptualised within the viewpoints of 'contextualised' and 'collaborative' creativity (Burnard, 2006; Csikszentmihalyi, 1996; Jeffery, 2005; John-Steiner, 2000; Miell & Littleton, 2004; Sawyer, 2003, 2006) where the social processes of group creativity are the focus (for a detailed discussion of collaborative creativity within this jazz ensemble see Kenny, 2014a).

Group perspectives

Within this jazz ensemble, creativity was viewed as lying between the sociocultural relationship between person, domain and field as adopted from Csikszentmihalyi's 'systems model' of creativity (Csikszentmihalyi, 1996). The interactions of these three elements were particularly illuminated within the jazz ensemble's public performances. During performance and in particular during improvisation sections, the jazz ensemble appeared to be in what Csikszentmihalyi refers to as 'flow' or an 'optimal experience' (1996).

In one performance the ensemble played 'Dr Jackle' as their finishing piece for the LJW term. It was instrumental only and a guest player from another ensemble joined the group on soprano saxophone. The norms of a jazz jamming session were in strong evidence during this performance. For instance, the players improvised at length, improvisations were respected through a physical turn of the body when not playing, and non-verbal gestures cued players' return to the tune. Jack and Jimmy's improvised duet on bass and drums during this tune indicated a comfortable and familiar style of performance as well as professional musician status within the group. Their loose, confident and creative playing was testament to a 25-year history of playing together which has been shown to result in high levels of 'creative collaboration' (John-Steiner, 2000; Miell & Littleton, 2004; Moran & John-Steiner, 2004). Although all of the players enjoyed improvising, they appeared more hesitant, particularly at entry points in the tune, and lacked the same level of confidence as the more experienced members.

A 'group flow state' (Sawyer, 2006) was evidenced within the performances where musical responses between players became more experimental; there was increased fluidity in passing on solos, greater use of non-verbal gestures to attend to conventions and more explicit peer approval (through behaviour such as bowing heads, nodding and occasional smiles). These moments in performance indicated an 'interactional synchrony of the performers' (Sawyer, 2003, p. 13) where the group appeared to be 'empathetically attuned' to each other (Seddon, 2005).

The creativity within the performances was of course a result of many rehearsals where there was a distinct practice of experimenting and playing creatively. This resonated with Davidson and Good's (2002) findings of a string quartet where they claimed 'spontaneous musical utterances' emerged from the 'interplay of stocks of musical knowledge'. Jimmy consistently encouraged the players to push boundaries in their playing during rehearsals. As well as giving instruction on how they might go about this, long monologue-style critiques were imparted including motivational or inspiring messages from jazz lore further demonstrated below:

> *Jimmy:* there's nothing safer than going up and just playing stuff that you've played a million times you know and unfortunately when you play like that a lot it becomes very drab no matter how technically good you are, it doesn't sound like it's going anywhere . . . let's face it you're not doing it for the money . . . if you were doing it for the money it'd be a different story you might have to worry about what people think about it . . . so you know you should do it from the point of view of some experimentation – there has to be some level of innovation. I remember Kenny Werner said once, 'the tradition of jazz is innovation'. That's the actual tradition of it and it's not reproducing stuff that you know over and over again. All the great jazz players – every one of them got slated probably at the time for certain things they were doing because they were doing something different . . . so you know you'll be dead long enough really.
>
> (LJWV1)

Just as jazz lore was used as a learning tool, Jimmy here again employed it as a mechanism to promote creativity in playing. Jimmy reminded the group of creative playing regularly and often used jazz lore to impart this message.

Individual perspectives

Members of the ensemble were very aware of the demands and challenges of achieving 'group creativity' and commented on this level of challenge frequently. This challenge was also viewed as a main reason to join and remain a member of the ensemble. The 'rules' of improvisation were learned through both community and musical practices. Just as the members recognised the need to work at creative playing, Jimmy asserted the need for knowledge to be present before creative practices could develop and commented, 'You hear some people doing free stuff and it's just random bullshit because they don't have any language to bring to it'.

Creativity and innovation (though improvisation) were seen as inseparable within the jazz ensemble. One of the members who was an accomplished Irish/folk musician but was relatively new to the jazz genre commented:

> The question in jazz is you don't know exactly what you are at, you don't work out solos, I haven't it pre-prepared . . . you just start and just hope that it works out and it generally does . . . and it works out better than you even imagined it would work . . . at this stage in my life when I play folk music, I'm generally within my comfort zone you know because I've been at it for so long but this is a whole new experience for me.
>
> (Enda)

Ensemble members referred to the immersive feeling of improvisatory performance often and Leona noted the spontaneity of jazz improvisation as, 'brilliant and you sometimes forget you are on stage'. These experiences of 'flow' (Csikszentmihalyi, 1996) were related primarily to performance experiences as opposed to rehearsals. Ryan related, 'There is a feeling of being immersed in the music and the moment – all focus is in the now – observing and experiencing being part of the music being made'. These 'peak experiences' (Csikszentmihalyi, 1996; Sawyer, 2003, 2006) were very evident in the video data of performances where long improvisatory passages formed a large part of their group music-making creative practices.

Jazz improvisation was considered by all members as a vital part of their creative practice with an overall consensus that their output of creativity was attributed to Jimmy's encouragement and facilitation. Ryan commented, 'Jimmy pushes you by use of free jazz – getting us to move beyond playing what is obvious' while Eric claimed, 'there's no feeling of playing within the comfort zone'. 'Challenge' had a strong association with creativity for the members. Although the jazz ensemble was a hobby for most of the players, the level of commitment was noteworthy. For instance, Leona related:

> We are always encouraged to come up not only with less traditional songs, but also with ideas for improvisation and arrangements. I find this very, very challenging. I am not naturally a creative person and (especially at the beginning) I struggled with the idea of changing things around and daring a little. I am more comfortable with it now, but it's still a lot of work.

While playing within a group context, the idea of 'personal creativity' was mentioned by all members. For instance, Leona stated that she felt she was not 'naturally a creative person', which would indicate a belief in creativity being innate. However, she also felt that due to sustained, creative participation within the group, her initial 'struggles' have become fewer, although admittedly creative playing is still 'a lot of work'.

The enjoyment of creative challenge within the ensemble's music-making was commented on by all members. Jimmy's emphasis on creative practice, which in turn influenced the group's approaches and attitudes, appeared to sustain the ensemble's membership. In addition, the experience of playing as a collective and engaging in collaborative creativity highly impacted on their sense of enjoyment in 'learning new stuff' (Jack) and sharing 'new ideas' (Beatrice) together as an ensemble. This resonated with Sawyer's description of 'collaborative emergence' where the whole is greater than the sum of its parts (2003, p. 12). Strong leadership, group membership, challenging playing and priority given to creative learning within the ensemble were all noted by the members as individual and collective reasons for the ensemble's success.

The need to consistently challenge the group and provide opportunities to engage in creative practices was especially important to the jazz ensemble. The creative practices of the ensemble then functioned as an interplay between individual and collaborative creativity where values such as privileging improvisation in performance and maintaining challenges in playing served to develop and build knowledge through leadership and collaboration.

Summary

Through investigating the community, musical and distinct creativity practices, key characteristics identified as unique to this community emerged. Through community practices the jazz ensemble formed and negotiated their membership and identities through their socio-musical interactions. This was obvious through delineated identities, leadership roles, a collective sense of group responsibility and the use of jazz lore as a means to induct members into a 'jazz world'.

Music-making within the ensemble relied on sustained built-up relationships formed through community practices. This was apparent through a constant interplay between leadership and shared learning, as well as formal and informal pedagogical approaches. Motivation to join and remain in the LJW emerged as reliant on musical challenge and opportunities for live performance. Creativity emerged as an important and distinctive feature of this jazz ensemble's identity and practices. Their creative practices were dependent on strong leadership but also collaborative effort where built-up knowledge and experiences in rehearsal led to increased improvisation and experimentation in performance.

In capturing the individual and group 'voices' of the jazz ensemble, this community was rooted in a micro practice but was located within the broader macro framework of group music-making contexts. The study of this jazz ensemble is as an important 'window' into how one distinct CoMP was developed and sustained through its practices.

4   A choral community

Ann:	Okay, 'Africa'.
Choir:	Yeah! (*some begin to hum, bounce*).
Ann:	I've told ye all to look at this on YouTube
Rianna:	Yeah, there's an eighties dance (*begins dancing in seat*)
Joey:	Oh, I didn't look at it
Ann:	You're honest, I could kill you but you're honest (*Jack laughs loudly*).

Take a page and pass it on, take a page and pass it on, take a page and pass it on (*Ann says it rhythmically, Chris begins tapping a beat on the table to the instruction*). *Music is handed out, lots of chatter, making lunch plans, sorting out pages of music.*

(CLYCV6[1])

The above extract from a choir rehearsal captures the sense of camaraderie experienced within this community of musical practice (CoMP) which appeared as a result of close-knit relationships built up over time. Ann, the choral director, gently scolded Joey in a jovial manner which caused Joey to react in laughter. The choir, due to the popularity of the piece, took the opportunity to mimic dances seen on YouTube and hum the tune expectantly. Furthermore, there was a musical interaction to be observed here between Ann and Chris, actual mother and son, where non-verbally, music was made informally and casually as sheet music was being passed around. All of these interactions demonstrated familiarity and closeness within the group where members were free to have fun with each other, chat and laugh together as well as with the choral director.

This chapter offers a window into the County Limerick Youth Choir (CLYC) as the second illustration of a CoMP. The age span of the choir ranged from 16 to 26 years (see Chapter 1 for contextual details). A significant majority of the 28-member choir were 18 years of age (12 members), most likely due to the age-related association with the last year of second-level education. The group

---

1 CLYCV6 refers to County Limerick Youth Choir Video 6. All video data is classified in this way, with the number indicating the sequence of the video recording session.

held a mix of four vocal sections – soprano, alto, tenor and bass, who also regularly split into eight parts for repertoire sung (for example, first soprano, second soprano, etc.). Eleven of the members were male (three basses and eight tenors) and the other 17 were female (seven sopranos and 10 altos), making a 73% to 27% split female to male. All members gained a place in the choir through an audition process which involved singing their chosen repertoire, sight-singing and vocal exercises. The choral director chose the members from this yearly process and had a waiting list of young people who could join if a space within a vocal part became available.

Findings from the youth choir's practices, seen as the group's way of doing things, are discussed here as community practices, musical practices and the distinctive practice of belonging which is particular to this CoMP. An analysis of group perspectives from the observation and video data collected over nine months offers distinct insights into the choir's 'musical world' (Finnegan, 2007). Findings from the participant logs as well as the interviews illuminate individual perspectives of the choir's practices within this discussion. The chapter provides an in-depth example from a youth choral group of how such musical communities can learn, interact, form identities and build relationships.

Community practices

The CLYC community practices were defined largely through social interactions such as learning processes, norms, routines, roles and membership. These community practices 'set the scene' of the CLYC and provided a holistic account of the community's *modus operandi*.

Group perspectives

The choir met weekly from 11am to 1pm on Saturday mornings in Limerick County Hall (which also housed the Limerick local government offices). Entry to the offices was quite restricted due to it being outside of working hours and due to this, access was gained through Ann, the choral director. In this way, the rehearsal space itself was regulated with a barrier to open entry. During the first 10 minutes of rehearsals latecomers were continually admitted and so the choral director in this physical manner was literally acting as the 'gatekeeper' to this CoMP.

The choir practised in a conference room on the lower-ground floor of the offices. Ann as choral director stood at the head of a large oval table at all rehearsals with an electric keyboard placed in front of her. The sopranos sat to the right of Ann, with altos at the end of the table, tenors to Ann's left and the basses further down on the same side. Due to the room layout, this was quite an unusual environment for a choral group, where often choirs might sit in sectional (sopranos/altos/tenors/basses) rows and would not normally practise in a conference room. This formation had consequences for social interactions. For example, as seen in Chapter 1, Parker found that 'sectional bonding' acted as 'social bonding' to a far greater degree than was found in the CLYC (Parker, 2010). While this was also evident in the study to some degree (to be discussed), the layout of the room meant that the vocal sections all faced each other and were in close proximity at any given time, allowing for increased opportunities for bonding across sections. The table layout also placed Ann metaphorically and symbolically 'at the same table' as the choir while retaining a leadership role at the 'top of the table' and behind an instrument.

As the choir was set up, funded and supported by the Limerick County Council Arts Office (see Chapter 1), the location of the rehearsals was quite emblematic. By physically providing the choir with rehearsal space in the council offices, the arts office was signifying a commitment to the choir and reinforcing its identity as specifically a council choir within a certain local community. Furthermore, it meant that the arts officer sometimes 'dropped in' on rehearsals to hear the choir, talk to them and arrange performance logistics with Ann.

The rehearsal sessions followed a very specific routine which always began with a vocal warm-up involving the whole choir. On average, over the 10 rehearsal sessions observed, these warm-ups ran for 12 minutes, where all members stood in their places as seen from the observational field notes below:

> *There is much talking . . . Ann returns from answering the door with two more members. Ann speaks over the students' talking, instructing them to redo a vocal exercise. She clears her throat, stands very straight, plays a few notes on the keyboard and with one hand gesture the choir begin singing together. They sing vocal exercises to a series of vowels, 'u-o-a' repeatedly going up and down the scale. There are references to a night out and some laughing exchanged between members between singing. The vocal exercises are done in unison with Ann accompanying on the keyboard. Ann instructs continually during the vocal exercises on such aspects as dynamics, mouth-shape, muscle support and pitch, verbally, as well as through hand gestures.*
>
> (CLYCV2)

This extract depicted the routine, interactions and behaviours associated with the practices of a CLYC warm-up. Ann took a strong leadership role as choral director where she led the vocal exercises to be done, the time spent on the exercises, the pace, level of challenge and ways to approach the exercises within the choir. A very traditional mode of teacher transmission was evident where the choir imitated, copied and followed instructions. Essentially the choir mimicked the behaviours and music-making of Ann who was seen to hold the expert knowledge here. Ann's non-verbal gestures and behaviours such as standing tall, clearing her throat, playing notes on the keyboard, using her arms to indicate dynamic changes, and drawing attention to a particular muscular area to focus on for vocal technique all acted as signifiers for the choir who implicitly knew these indicated a readiness to begin or move on in the exercises. The choir responded to all of this and the switch in exercises with great fluidity and immediacy, indicating a shared history of this type of engagement. For Bithell (2014, p. 112), a choral warm-up 'functions as a ritual that re-establishes the group's identity'. For this choir, the sense of the familiar and routine within these warm-up practices remained constant throughout the 10 rehearsals.

There were interesting social interactions to be observed in the above example with much chatter and laughter between the vocal sections and across vocal sections (while Ann went to answer the door, as well as during breaks in the vocal exercises). Such interaction was facilitated by the rehearsal formation where the members could all see each other while singing. While there was much joking and laughter within rehearsals, there was also a clear readiness to begin singing if instructed in this way with the choir often breaking their conversations mid-sentence. The shared activity of singing together and sense of group responsibility, coupled with a shared history of working in this way, characterised these interactions. Ann also engaged in some of these social exchanges and at one point in this same rehearsal questioned, 'did you have a good night?', also indicating a strong social life outside of the choir between members. In addition, Ann often demonstrated a nurturing attitude towards the members during these beginning warm-ups such as asking members how they were and making room when others arrived late. It was also very regular for Ann to chat to the choir informally between rehearsing short exercises.

The strong leadership from the choral director was further evidenced in the extract below where we see Ann again taking control of the repertoire circulated, choral direction and at one point chastising, 'stop flinging them around'. Due to the language of the piece, however, Ann does look for group input and support in learning the new piece, asking, 'who's good at Spanish?'. From the extract, the members were reluctant to take on the role of leading the language learning and suggested other people while Mona avoided a response altogether. On the one hand this may indicate a lack of confidence in the language, skill level required or age-related embarrassment at being singled out, but may also indicate a reluctance to take on any leadership role that so obviously rested with Ann in the choir:

> *Ann*:   Who's good at Spanish?
> *Marianne*:   Amy
> *All students start laughing and talking as they pass around music sheets*
> *Amy*:   I'm so brutal
> *Sharon*:   Mona, Mona
> *Nathan*:   Where is John Keane when you need him?
> *Ann*:   Mona do you have Spanish up to that?
> *No definite response from Mona. One of the photocopies flies off the table onto the floor and a student climbs under to get it*
> *Ann*:   (tutting) Aw now. Okay who doesn't have music yet and stop flinging them around . . .
> *Some members start laughing*

Ann: Okay for the moment (returns to keyboard) I'm just going to do it on 'bom' because I want to get the rhythm ok? I'm going to count in three . . . (members have got quieter) so all the men are together . . . the men, I'm only joking
Laughter

Ann: (plays notes) 'El Gavilan' (Carrillo) We can do the opening . . .
All four parts read music and sing their sections together on 'bom'.

(CLYCV3)

From the above, social interaction is evidenced as being a large part of the choir's community practices. For instance, the members took opportunities for much laughter and chatting in between singing as discussed previously with the warm-ups. Ann too joined in the fun with a quip about the male vocal sections, 'the men, I'm only joking'. Such a joke indicated a recognised group identity and segregated gender parts as well as a reference to the group's youth. However, once it was time to get down to the business of singing, the choir become quieter and focused on the task at hand; in this case singing 'El Gavilan' to 'bom'. In this manner, the hard work of music-making always took precedence over social interaction for the group and was approached seriously.

The CLYC had a significant performance in Éigse[2] Michael Hartnett (a Limerick County Council Poetry, Arts & Literary Festival dedicated to the Limerick-born poet). The extract below sees a goal-orientated focus to the rehearsal due to the pressure of upcoming gigs as well as organisational issues surrounding the performances:

Ann: Okay, I know ye think we probably have enough for the Éigse thing, but we don't have enough . . . we have managed to get a song that Bill Whelan wrote by putting one of Michael Hartnett's poems to music so it is really really nice and he has been really nice in giving it to us, and emailed me the music . . . so it will need a soprano and a tenor and a violin and piano so it will be nice to have it in there as well. So already we have two sopranos who volunteered, are there any other sopranos who would like to give it a go . . . speak now or forever hold your peace (laughter) . . . Evelyn, would you like to give it a go?
Evelyn: Eh, I'll try it
Ann: Well what we can do, you see we have the 'Dixit' as well so whoever wants to do them will have to get copies and work on them and we can split it okay?
Ann: Okay, tenors?
Nathan: I'll try it
Ann: Okay, you'll give it a go, how is your Irish?

2 'Éigse' is the Irish language word for 'poetry'.

Nathan: Ar fheabhas [trans: Excellent]! (laughter from choir)

Ann: Ta súil agam [trans: I hope so] (more laughter)

Nathan: I'll find out on Wednesday . . . how high does it go?

Ann: (flicks through music) Not very high . . . we'll come in as a group as well, do you know what I mean, we'll come in on the chorus, I know it is more music for ye to do but . . . I'll get more copies when Jill comes in. Okay, let's run through 'Cantemus' now as we need that for Friday.

Conor: Oh, I think I have a gig that night . . .

Ann: Can ye not rearrange it . . . no? Do the two of ye (looks at Chris and Ursula) have a gig that night? (They shake their heads) No, okay . . . 'Cantemus', 1, 2, 3 . . .

                                                                              (CLYCV9)

From the field notes, it was clear that the choir were busy and in demand. The strong reputation of the choir was also evident in being granted new Irish contemporary music from well-known Irish composer/producer Bill Whelan. As well as having a heavy performance schedule within the choir, there was also evidence here of outside busy musical lives as well. Conor explains he has another gig the night of one performance and Ann double-checks with two other members if they have one scheduled also. Here the overlapping membership in multiple and overlapping music communities was brought to light.

The extract also revealed a very informal and shared method of assigning solo parts to singers. The choir members were seen volunteering, 'I'll try it', as opposed to auditioning for the sections. Ann stressed that, 'whoever wants to do them will have to get copies and work on them', emphasising the need to take on responsibility for their own learning here. This was all carried out in a very casual and non-competitive way with reminders of support from the overall group through Ann, 'we'll come in as a group'.

Individual perspectives

The participant logs and interviews provided individual perspectives on the choir's experiences, opinions and understandings of their community practices. Thus, these data sets complemented the group perspectives of the observational and video data.

Motivations to join the choir stemmed from: having a previous link with the choral director, the good reputation of the choir, a love of singing, the draw of social interaction and the level of challenge involved, as seen in some of the log entries below:

I had always wanted to join the choir after being a member of Ann's Children's Choir. I had seen them perform and knew I was going to join as soon as I turned 16!

                                                                              (Conor)

I joined CLYC because I was very interested in music and wanted to enhance singing lessons.

(Kristen)

I expected to feel like part of a group and was looking forward to singing with others.

(Sam)

It was interesting to note many of the choral members held previous membership of other choirs led by Ann, and in particular her children's choir. Hence, there was a feeling of progression from one choral community to another, linked through the choral director. As well as this, the connection appeared to enable the members to hear the choir live ahead of joining through such events as shared choral concerts and so this often influenced their decision to be a part of the youth choir. For instance, Emer noted, 'I had heard CLYC perform a good few times. They always sounded amazing and I really wanted to be a part of that amazing sound!'

From the focus group interviews, it was clear that music teachers had a significant influence on the members' reasons for joining the choir. Three of the members mentioned singing teachers (one of which was Ann, the choral director) while Karen also mentioned the school music teacher as being the motivating force to audition for the choir. This resonated with findings from Pitts who claims, 'the attention offered to emerging musicians by their instrumental teachers can be one of the strongest influences on musical development' (2012, p. 92). However, Pitts also writes of the multiple and varied routes into musical participation which were also found within this study. For instance, Joey joined through encouragement from his friendship with Kristen who was already in the choir while Chris, being Ann's son, became a member in large part for pragmatic family reasons (to not be home alone). What was most interesting here was that all of the members were motivated to join the choir through interwoven and intersecting music communities. Through these connections and relationships, they gained access to the musical world of the CLYC.

Ann felt that commitment from the choir members was key to its success, claiming at interview, 'if somebody is going to come to audition for a choir that meets on a Saturday morning they must be committed, so that in itself leads to success'. The choir members overwhelmingly wrote in their logs about the importance of overall group responsibility to the choir. Nancy maintained, 'everyone must do their job and play their part and everyone is of equal importance' while Conor similarly noted, 'we all work together to make something great . . . . Equality is key to us working as a group'. Here we can see that as part of the community's practices, maintaining equity and a sense of accountability to the choir was important with an emphasis placed on working collaboratively.

There were significant differences recorded, however, between the established members of the choir and 'newcomers', illustrating a diversity of roles defined through community practices. The established members related feelings of confidence, both socially and musically, as well as a sense of 'belonging' in the group, being part of a 'big family', 'needed' (Amy) and 'able to assist' (Noreen). Ann was often mentioned as assisting with confidence in the logs and focus group interview. Kristen related:

> I feel like I have developed a lot vocally since I began . . . I am also more confident participating in the social side of choir, whereas I was quite shy and introverted when I first began. I believe that this self-confidence comes from both the security of the group and the confidence Ann has in us as individuals.

The newer members, however, did not have this sense yet of being at the centre of the choir, but rather wrote about 'still learning' and the need to 'catch up' (Rianna). Nancy initially felt that 'a lot of the people that were in the choir already knew each other and so it took me a few months to get to know people'. Nancy felt this sense of 'peripheral participation' (Wenger, 1998) was heightened due to her being 'from the country' and so feeling outside a 'city group' that knew each other. This lack of confidence and 'belonging' were both musical and social then where Elisha also pointed out she was, 'just getting to know people and getting to know the music'. Hence, these 'newcomers' were engaging in a form of apprenticeship learning that involved both musical and social interactions to acquire a 'feel for the game' to assimilate into this particular 'field of practice' (Bourdieu, 1977, 1984, 1990, 2002).

Groups within the choir that knew each other well socialised regularly after choir rehearsal, often going for lunch and progressing onto other rehearsals for other musical groups they were involved with. Due to these established relationships, Ann felt that newcomers experienced some difficulties upon entering such a close-knit choral community, 'certainly the younger ones, the newer ones coming in will stick together . . . eventually they fit in you know but it doesn't happen overnight'. She felt this was often age-related as newcomers were invariably entering at age 16 and the more established members were older (up to 26 years of age). Ann noted that choral trips away aided a coming together in this regard which mirrored findings within the participant logs. Parker in her study of an adolescent high school choir similarly found that trips helped to 'fortify the choir team' (Parker, 2014, p. 30).

With regard to leadership, Ann as choral director was viewed as the distinct leader in the group. Her style was described as 'friendly', 'engaging', 'kind' and 'understanding' while also being 'firm' and 'diligent'. The members in their logs and at interview invariably noted a huge respect for Ann as someone they all looked up to. She was seen as both a nurturer and expert who strove for high standards in the choir, thus acting as a key motivator for members. This resonated with the US choral study where 'choir teachers were highly influential because their marriage of high expectations and compliments encouraged adolescents to mirror their behavior' (Parker, 2014, p. 29). The striking elements of the CLYC responses in this regard were summarised eloquently by Kristen, an established member of the choir:

We all look up to Ann. She rarely has to give out because we all want to do our best for her. I think this stems from the faith she seems to have in us all individually . . . because she has the confidence you can – you can. She is never short of ideas for us and is always looking for us to do bigger and better things. I think everyone in the choir has the utmost respect and appreciation for her.

In summary, the CLYC developed and sustained community practices through their participation and collaboration. The community practices of the choir can be characterised as the practices of: maintaining a goal-orientated focus, interplay between leadership and group responsibility, integration of musical and social interactions, promoting close-knit relationships and defined roles by seniority.

Musical practices

The observation and video data consistently revealed familiarity and fluidity in the choir's musical practices where a scaffolded approach to learning incorporated sight-singing from notation, guided instruction from the choral director, focused vocal section work and shared memory. Musical interactions were characterised by certain routines, behaviours, cues and gestures which were carried out with a strong sense of shared history between the members.

Group perspectives

The choral repertoire was always decided by Ann, as was the order they were rehearsed. During the fieldwork period, 20 choral pieces were rehearsed across classical, folk and contemporary classical genres ranging from pieces from Sergei Rachmaninov ('Bogoroditsc Devo') to Jean Sibelius ('Be Still My Soul', 'Glockenmelodie') to György Orbán ('Daemon Irrepit Callidus') to Eric Whitacre ('Lux Arumque', 'Sleep'). Irish composers such as Charles Villiers Stanford ('Bluebird') and contemporary composer Bill Whelan ('Dán do Lara') were also included. This eclectic mix of composers also meant the languages sung by the CLYC were varied, with the choir singing in Russian, German, French, Irish, English and Latin often in the space of one rehearsal.

The leadership in music-making from Ann in her role as choral director was apparent in choosing the repertoire but also in the immediacy of the choir responding to Ann's lead and instructions within rehearsals and performances. This was very evident in the warm-ups depicted earlier but extended beyond this. Musical gestures and cues from Ann were as important as verbal instructions within the choir and often captured the choir's attention more responsively than actual talk. The extract from the video field notes below illuminates the choir's routine and practices when singing a familiar piece of music:

The choir are rehearsing 'Magnum Mysterium' (Lauridsen). The choir are standing not in the usual formation of choral sections but mixed-up parts as instructed by Ann. Ann gives some instruction, plays chords on the keyboard and conducts the choir in. Some members sing from music, others do not. The choir watch Ann intently while she conducts, instructs and gestures during the singing.

(CLYCV1)

Here, the choir stood when Ann felt they were ready to sing the song as a performance piece. In the standing, the choir appeared more focused and to take themselves more seriously. The choir in the videoed extract sang predominantly from memory, indicating a shared history and collective knowledge of the piece. Musical signifiers or gestures from the choral director were employed to stay together and add interpretative nuances to the song such as clicking, singing vocal section entries and playing notes on the keyboard occasionally to re-establish pitch. As well as this, the choir had to work in mixed vocal sections, without music. Ann frequently used this pedagogy with the choir to challenge their singing, promoting group responsibility as well as individual responsibility to hold each vocal line. These musical practices were carried out in a group task-based collaborative manner where each member had a part to play and 'belonged' to the overall sound.

Just as the choir responded musically (in their singing) to Ann's directions, cues and gestures, the choir's reaction to singing 'Daemon Irrepit Callidus' (Orbán) in the extract below also saw the choir respond physically to music-making:

'Daemon Irrepit Callidus' (Orbán). Choir really attack it – enjoy it, familiar, some smiling between them, little bit of bouncing, dancing. Due to music, impact of meter. Ann: 'Okay it sounds like (imitates roaring), it still needs to be tuneful!' (laughter) Jokes and laughter in reaction to music and singing. Ann continued to stop and start, instruct, conduct. Singers enjoy again, Chris (bass) jumps up and down a little, laughter, members bounce along to particularly rhythmic sections, singers appear to know this song well.

(CLYCV6)

From the above, it was clear that the choir were thoroughly enjoying the act of music-making collectively through their exchange of smiles, bouncing and dancing to the rhythmic sections of the piece. Their familiarity with the music, the vocal parts and each other appeared to allow them this freedom to enjoy the music-making, leave the score and sing as one cohesive sound. Ann too appeared to enjoy this piece and although is critical – 'it still needs to be tuneful' – this was delivered in a jovial way and encouraged much shared laughter within the choir.

While such enjoyment was evident in familiar pieces of music, new or less familiar pieces to be learned went through a different music-making process. In such instances, Ann guided the new learning through instruction, gestures, singing with the vocal sections and playing the keyboard to aid note learning. The pedagogy engaged in was very much based on a scaffolding process where Ann began with one vocal section (typically sopranos as they often had the main tune) followed by the other vocal sections to build up and learn a difficult passage in the music. Ann first established the main melody and following this attended to various vocal skills or techniques. Often one aspect of the singing was focused on in a rehearsal, for example breathing, where Ann taking control would call out over the singing where to take and not to take breaths. In addition to this leadership role, Ann often passed on group responsibility within vocal sections such as decision-making between members on where to take breaths.

It was very apparent within rehearsals how much the choir relied on competent sight-singing from its members. With new pieces of music the notes were learned very quickly and attempted straight away, indicating much previous collective musical knowledge and experience of approaching music in this way. At one rehearsal, an alto left the room and upon her return, her fellow alto pointed to the bar of music they were on. No words were exchanged, the singing continued and seamlessly the alto was able to join her vocal section in sight-singing due to her musical knowledge but also the aid given from her vocal section member. Within this fleeting exchange, the importance of collegiality, collaboration and group responsibility was evident.

Throughout the music-making in rehearsals, the choir and choral director repeatedly evaluated their singing. This was seen in Ann's consistent tweaking and instruction but also in the way the group laughed at their mistakes and adjusted their singing to meet the desired goal. Further evidence of this group evaluation can be seen in the extract below:

> *The choir are rehearsing 'Sleep' (Whitacre)*
> Ann: (during singing) Watch your ths . . . watch the pitch . . . (plays chords now and again when notes need adjusting) . . . keep the ps together . . . more crescendo
> *Choir very familiar with music here, Ann uses the keyboard very little, singers use the notation less than before, reference only. Finish singing.*
> Ann: Yeah.
> Choir: (laugh, look around, joke to one another)
> *Marianne in the sopranos leans over and says something to Ann*
> Ann: (to sopranos) Who was doing it?
> Kristen: Everyone, all the sopranos, we were all doing it.
> Ann: It just changed, the quality of it just changed somewhere . . .
> Marianne: I stopped singing about two bars in . . .
> Ann: That's fine, if you stop, stop. I mean I said to ye before (to whole choir) if you stop stay stopped, don't come back in, if it's meant to be getting quieter and quieter, don't just suddenly get loud again . . .
> Choir: (laughter)
>
> (CLYCV7)

From the above, it was clear that the group were actively listening and evaluating their singing just as the choral director did. The choir laughed when they finished singing, knowing that they were not up to standard. Senior member Marianne went further to inform Ann of a difficulty with the soprano line which Ann then turned to address. The sopranos were quick to take on group responsibility with Kristen, another senior member remarking, 'we were all doing it'. The choir were very much involved in musically problem-solving what went wrong and Ann used a point of technique (decrescendo) with one vocal part as a learning tip to the whole choir. This was carried out in a jovial way with the choir laughing at the thought of the mistake of getting loud on a decrescendo.

Within the two performances observed, the choir again relied heavily on Ann to lead the music performance practices. At each performance it was Ann who gave the starting notes, conducted and led the choir on and off stage. The performances differed greatly of course in the music-making of rehearsal in that there was no stopping, adjusting or instruction. The choir sang through their pieces in full, relying on Ann's guidance and the built-up, collective knowledge and shared memory of rehearsals. The performances were taken very seriously by the choir, made apparent in their behaviours on stage which were more formal and focused than in a rehearsal.

One performance saw the choir sing amongst other local choirs from the Limerick/Clare region in the mid-west of Ireland as part of a cancer awareness fundraiser. Although the venue was an inflatable stage at an outside venue in County Clare, seemingly at odds with the CLYC identity and genre of singing (in that the acoustic was poor, flashing coloured lights lit the stage and essentially the setup appeared to be more suited to popular bands), the choir performed four pieces in a very formal manner led by Ann. They wore black, stood tall in a formation of two rows and sang from memory. The extract below captures part of the performance:

> *Ann plays notes on the keyboard, walks over to the choir and conducts a performance of 'Sleep' (Whitacre). The choir sing from memory, looking at Ann throughout. The audience are attentive and when the choir finish, clap loudly. Some choir members turn towards each other and exchange some smiles. Ann closes the music in front of her and looks up at the choir for a moment before taking out the next piece.*

> (CLYCV11)

The choir were seen following Ann intently throughout the singing here as well as relying on shared memory and knowledge from rehearsing. Ann is very much the leader in performance seen in such behaviours as: reshuffling the choir before the piece begins (for a particular sound and blend depending on the music sung), gesturing, getting the notes from the keyboard, and ultimately starting, guiding and finishing the singing. Although Ann had the music in front of her, it was obvious that she did not need it in performance and turns the pages without looking down, knowing the music intimately. Thus, just as the choir watch her direction throughout the performance, Ann too reciprocates in watching them closely, maintaining close contact with the choir throughout.

From the performance of 'Sleep' in the extract, the choir also appeared to self-evaluate just as was evidenced in rehearsal earlier. Instead of remarking, however, due to the performance platform, this was carried out through non-verbal gestures. For example, some choir members turned to each other and smiled during the applause. Ann equally acknowledged the end of the piece by staring straight at them during the applause, again retaining close contact with her choir rather than turning to the audience to receive the applause.

Individual perspectives

The logs and interviews aimed to capture insights into the individual members' musical practices. It emerged that of the 11 log respondents, 10 of them were engaged in musical activities outside of the CLYC and three of them noted spending over 10 hours a week participating in musical communities. These strong musical identities ranged in their multi-membership within school choirs, musical societies, stage schools, bands, church choirs and orchestras.

Eight of the 11 respondents practised specific CLYC material for one hour a week outside of rehearsal time while the others' practice time ranged from two to three hours. Within practising habits, it was clear that listening was a significant technique for the members, with each respondent noting it in their logs. Technological supports such as iPods, YouTube videos as well as recording and playback facilites were referenced widely as an integral aspect of practising. Throughout the entries the members rehearsed their own lines but also aimed to hear the other lines in relation to the overall sound. Conor notes, 'I usually sit at the piano with the music and work through my line, noting any difficulties. Then sometimes I record the other lines on the electric piano and then try and sing my line accurately to the others'. In this way, although individually practising, the members were still cognisant of a holistic choral sound.

When writing about the influence of the choir on their practising habits, there was a strong emphasis on group responsibility. For instance, Amy wrote, 'makes me want to try harder because other people in the choir try and I want to put in the work they do'. There was an overwhelming sense of hard work and progression in learning evidenced within individual logs. The community itself also held high musical expectations of its members as related in interview. Members recollected feeling scared and intimidated when they joined due to the reputation and exclusive nature of the choir. For instance, Joey related, 'I had no idea what I was doing for the first couple of months' and Chris recalled, 'my first few weeks were just me completely quiet'. However, through immersion and learning from others they felt they had all scaled steep learning curves and that their preconceptions were challenged. Karen stated:

When I joined I was expecting to be intimidated because I knew people that were in it already and I'd heard about them and it was supposed to be a brilliant choir . . . it was so scary getting used to it because you're like oh I don't want them to think I'm not good enough but then you just start to blend in and you become comfortable and it's just a really nice environment to be in.

Joey similarly claimed, 'Eventually it just clicked, it was strange how all of a sudden just being submersed in it worked'. In this way, the members were very aware of the time required to build knowledge and relationships to become a full member of the choir, essentially being inculcated and thereby influencing community and musical practices.

The members were very clear about the musical benefits membership in the choir gave them. Musically, Ann argued that the choir trained the members very well in terms of harmonic, rhythmic and pitch awareness as well as increased sight-singing skills. The confidence-building through these musical practices had a positive effect on the members taking music up as an exam subject in secondary school and for some members, music onto third-level education. Therefore, the choir fostered musical practices that were able to translate and overlap into intersecting music communities, such as school-based music. The choir members too felt an increased musical awareness in areas such as pitch and sight-singing as well as mentioning being more comfortable and confident in singing. These benefits were often associated with group singing as opposed to singing on one's own. Marianne claimed at interview, 'pitch I think is a big thing in choir because when you're singing solo you kind of get away with it as such, like it's just you and you're not affecting anyone else but when you're singing in a choir everyone has to be in pitch with each other'.

This strong musical practice also impacted on the members' sense of musical identity. It emerged that four of the five focus group interviewees attended voice lessons with Ann outside of the choir. Of those interviewed, music was viewed as a central part of their lives with multiple memberships in music communities, whether as a hobby or career choice. Kristen felt it was such a significant part of her life that she had recently left a college course in medicine in favour of music. She revealed:

> I went to do medicine in Cork at the start of the year. I was like just going to keep music up as a hobby but then when I got down there I realised I hate medicine. So now I've taken an entire gap year and I'm going to do music now in college. I kind of dropped everything I was aiming for to go back and do music.

Ann was continually making evaluative judgements on the choir's singing and implementing changes. As well as these immediate evaluations, Ann also revealed at interview a more reflective process that she engaged in. Ann felt that while awards won were affirming, there was still a lot of room for self-evaluation which was crucial to the choir's continued development. She stated:

> I'll always feel there might be one or two things that sometimes I let go during rehearsal and in actual performance I'll hear it, I'll start being more aware of it and I'll regret that I didn't do something about it. So this is a growing thing on my part, I have to kind of always really think about what I want from the finished project.

The choir too engaged in self as well as group evaluation. This emphasis on attentive listening, akin to the choral director, was viewed as crucial to the overall choral sound and group responsibility within the CLYC. As well as this, evaluation through performance itself and audience reaction were recognised at interview, for example Kristen commented, 'You listen and think – oh we need to get better'. There was also a preoccupation with keeping up the strong reputation of the choir. Joey explained, 'we have a good reputation, people are spreading our name and they want us to perform'.

The shared goal of performance was seen as crucial to their musical practices where it was claimed: 'you have a goal to go for' (Karen) and 'people wouldn't see the point in coming if there was nothing to work towards' (Joey). Kristen also pointed out the heightened musical output that performance allowed, claiming, 'I think that some of the moments we've had in performances have been the best that we've ever sang. They bring out the best in the choir'.

From the logs, personal fulfilment, a sense of togetherness as a group and achievement were the main types of feelings associated with performance. On a personal level, members referred to performance as 'an amazing feeling' (Kristen) and being 'in a completely different world' (Noreen). Amy related, 'It makes me feel amazing, I feel such a rush when I'm with them! Creating such a beautiful sound! It can pull you out of any bad mood, it lifts my spirits'. This had strong echoes with the concept of 'flow' (Csikszentmihalyi, 1996; Sawyer, 2003, 2006b) where participants in creative activity such as choral performance can have such an immersive 'peak experience' (see Chapter 1).

A feeling of togetherness in performance was strong amongst the respondents. Both Suzie and Joey commented on the 'great' feeling it brought 'to feel important in a group of people' (Suzie) and that performing brought 'a real feeling of togetherness and dependency, it's just a different feeling than performing alone in that way' (Joey). This related significantly to other data sets where a sense of 'belonging' was evident as important to the group (discussed further in the next section). Being quite task-focused as a choir, it was not surprising that performance aided a feeling of achievement amongst members.

To summarise, the emerging musical practices that were most significant within the CLYC findings included: an emphasis on performance, the choir's use of and reactions to musical signifiers, gestures and cues, learning through the strong leadership role of the choral director, group input, and engaging in self and group evaluation as well as maintaining strong musical identities that overlapped with music communities outside of the choir itself.

Distinctive practice: belonging

The CLYC throughout the data analysis consistently revealed a close-knit, family-like character. This distinctive practice of 'belonging' in the group manifested itself in both musical and social interactions. The membership within the CLYC involved interrelated roles and identities delineated through such aspects as gender, age, leadership and seniority. All of these facets of membership overlapped and complemented one another to create a distinctive practice of belonging within the choir.

Group perspectives

The very structure and formation of the choir's rehearsal space promoted a sense of 'belonging' in that the choir were in close proximity, facing each other, and the choral director was at the 'same table'. The CLYC members, due to the choir's nature as an SATB choir (soprano, altos, tenors and basses), held membership roles within the choir as a whole but also roles within their vocal sections. These vocal section roles were evident physically in where the members sat and stood for performance, separated by gender simply due to vocal type but also distinguished musically through the singing of different melodic lines. In rehearsing 'Bogoroditsye Dyevo' (Rachmaninov) below we see the vocal sections going over lines separately and then coming together to sing the piece through:

> *Ann goes through a section of music from 'Bogoroditsye Dyevo' with sopranos, altos, tenors and basses one by one. At times, somebody in a vocal part asks for a note or phrase to be repeated. Ann instructs each section where to improve one by one. Then all parts sing together. Once singing stops there is a slight laugh over holding the final note. Ann smiles, 'thank you and again'*
>
> (CLYCV4)

This scaffolding process of rehearsing, evident where vocal sections learned their sections separately to input into the collective sound, set immediate parameters for the members' input into the choir. As such, 'belonging' to the group relied on individual input, vocal section input and then overall choir input for the shared goal of music-making to happen and lead ultimately to performance output. Evidence of the group self-evaluating was also revealed where we see the choir laughing at the attempt to sing together, which Ann smiles at. Collectively, the choir heard when something sounded wrong, indicating a sense of group responsibility (also seen previously in earlier sections).

The seating arrangements facilitated a lot of 'sectional bonding' (Parker, 2010) between vocal parts and as a result gender. This created certain social groupings but also social activities between sections were also evident throughout the observations, where members across sections chatted, laughed and could be heard making social plans for after-choir practice all of the time. In this case, the social groups appeared to be more age-related and linked with seniority within the choir where there was a distinct difference marked socially between members who were in college, in their leaving certificate examination[3] year and the members younger than this age. This resonated strongly with the delineation of 'oldtimers' and 'newcomers' as participants of a community of practice (CoP) (Wenger, 1998).

This focus on school examinations in the young people's lives dominated their talk within rehearsal and also in their exchanges with Ann as choral director. Often

---

3   The leaving certificate is the terminal state examination of post-primary education in Ireland. It is used for entry into third-level education, further education, employment and training.

extra rehearsals were negotiated around study schedules; Ann made enquiries about their progress and appeared concerned for their wellbeing with exam stress. In this way, Ann took on a nurturing role as demonstrated in the extract here:

> *Ann*: Okay, let's have a look at 'Lux Aurumque' . . . this is Friday as well so (plays chords, put out hands to conduct). Emily, you try it? (Emily wipes nose and nods) Are you smothered? God, ye're all smothered, lots of vitamin C and echinacea now please (claps hands). (Choir laugh) Are you Leaving Cert as well? Yeah it's unbelievable.
>
> *Joey*: Yeah I'm allergic to it (laughter)
>
> (CLYCV10)

From the extract above, Ann reassured the members, encouraged them to take care of themselves and eased exam tension through laughter with the group. In this way, there was an overwhelming feeling of 'belonging' and family-like exchanges, where Ann took up a nurturing or carer role in this close-knit community.

A sense of fun and laughter encouraged this sense of 'belonging'. Jokes and shared laughter predominantly centred on the music-making itself often led by Ann or senior members of the choir. For instance, Ann reacting to the speeding up of a piece commented, 'Let's have a race, who won?' (CLYCV10) and Chris commented on his hoarseness, 'My voice is decayed like' (CLYCV8). Due to the disciplined, hardworking nature of the rehearsals, the established members and choral director almost permitted times for laughter and jovial attitudes towards singing to balance the task-orientated focus of the rehearsals.

The 'oldtimers' (Lave & Wenger, 1991; Wenger, 1998) or established members of the choir also revealed themselves through other practices such as talking to Ann more frequently than newer members, taking the lead for vocal sections, volunteering for solo sections and organising travel to performances. For instance, Chris was with the choir for over five years and was also the son of the choral director. His senior membership coupled with family ties cast Chris into an assistant-type role where Ann regularly relied on him to answer the door and make extra photocopies. The extract below reveals an interesting instance where Chris made judgements about the choir's rehearsing:

> 'Daemon' (Orban)
> *Everyone looks at music or shares music except for Chris, appears to sing from memory. Singing breaks up halfway through the song and everyone laughs.*
>
> *Ann*: (looking at Chris) Chris, you forgot to come in there . . .
>
> *Chris*: Oh, I stopped singing 'cause it was terrible.
>
> *Choir*: (Laughter)
>
> *Ann*: It was not terrible! (laughs) I have to keep going, okay, can you stand up and get into your groups please . . . Ye shouldn't need to look at the music, if ye have to, just now and again.
>
> (CLYCV8)

Here, Chris took on a leadership and evaluative role (normally held by his mother, the choral director), making the decision to stop singing as 'it was terrible'. Chris delivered this evaluation in a very laidback manner but was also letting Ann know that his stopped singing was not a mistake. This was laughed at by the choir and Ann was quick to reassure the choir and move on with the singing.

As a local government-funded choir, the group had a significant role to play in the local government-run festival 'Éigse' (referenced earlier in this chapter), indicating 'belonging' to a particular local context. This particular performance highlighted the strong link and identity the choir had with local government. Here, the arts officer and choral director worked together and shared decisions within rehearsals to reach a performance-ready piece of work. The relationship between the arts officer, choral director and choir members was revealed as familiar and collegial where the arts officer, Jill, was welcomed into rehearsals and inputted into rehearsal as further revealed below:

> *Ann*:   Bar 21, okay? And just so you know, Bill Whelan wrote this poem for his daughter Lara and Lara is going to be there (*choir look up, surprised*). No pressure! (laughter)
>
> *Jill*:   Coming all the way from Australia (laughter)
>   *Choir look shocked.*
>
> *Ann*:   This is for Friday. Okay . . .
>
> *Jill*:   No, no, they are going to be wonderful!
>
> *Ann*:   I know that, they always are (plays notes and raises one hand to conduct, gives notes to each part)
>   *Choir sing 'Dan Do Lara' (Whelan)*
>
> *Ann*:   Thank you (turns to Jill)
>
> *Jill*:   Yeah, that was lovely.
>
> *More discussion follows between Ann and Jill on what to do next. A lot of this is prepared in the moment, coming up with ideas as they move through poems and music.*
>
> (CLYCV8)

Within this exchange Ann and Jill both shared their high expectations for the choir and fondness for the choir itself with Jill exclaiming, 'they are going to be wonderful' and Ann responding, 'they always are'. The extract also revealed the shared creative decisions between Ann and Jill as well as the respect they had for each other in this process.

The member holding the most seniority within the choir of course was the choral director, Ann. This leadership role was never in question and this manifested itself through conducting, evaluating, instructing, making decisions, choosing repertoire and essentially holding the expert knowledge within the group. Ann was also a distinctly different member of the group, being outside of the age limit and being the only paid member for this leadership. Despite these obvious teacher/learner roles assumed within such a setup, Ann very much 'belonged' and this was evident in shared smiles, laughter and jokes. Furthermore, Ann relied on the choir's input and promoted a sense of inclusion in rehearsing, as seen in requests from the choir to play certain sections again which Ann always welcomed.

Thus, Ann encouraged a sense of group responsibility in her comments, as seen in the example here:

> *Ann:*   Ye can look at it at home, ye can practise it at home. We have too much to do, we have a lot to do this year. Study it. It is not enough to just look at it for two hours on a Saturday. It is not enough. Learn it. We should just be colouring in here, not going through yer lines at this stage.
> *Choir do not respond, glance at each other, pass music around. Shuffle, guilty looks.*
>
> (CLYCV4)

From the above, there was a strong sense of togetherness and membership promoted by Ann, through the consistent use of the words 'ye' and 'we'. The choir responded guiltily to the criticism, clearly feeling a sense of group responsibility and accountability here.

A distinctive practice of 'belonging' was what overwhelmingly characterised the identity, relationships and membership of the choir. This was evident in their chatting and joking which ranged from topics on performances, music they listened to and exam pressures to what they were going to do for lunch. It was also evident musically in their sectional responsibility for lines as well as inputting into a collective choral sound. Membership was wholly reliant on socio-musical relationships where both social and musical aspects of the choir facilitated identity and role formation.

Individual perspectives

Relationships within the CLYC were seen as crucial to its identity and success within the interviews and logs. The members related feelings of 'belonging', associating the choir with familial characteristics and comparing the choral director to a parental figure. Members relied on close relationships to feel a sense of 'belonging' to the group.

Ann at interview pointed out the centrality of good relationships within the choir and the need to leave room for social interactions within rehearsal time. She mentioned the familiarity members had with each other outside of the choir due to participation in overlapping musical communities such as musical theatre, school, bands and church choirs. Ann spoke of striving to ensure the members were happy and felt a sense of 'belonging' at rehearsal, stating, 'it's a Saturday morning, so you want them to feel that they are coming to some place where they can be themselves, where they're comfortable and yet they can enjoy singing'.

Being a choir for 16–26-year-olds, age-related differences were capitalised on in the choir where an apprenticeship, peer-learning culture was encouraged by the choral director. Ann believed:

you'll always get the 17-year-olds going to hang around together, the 22-year-olds are going to hang around together but when they are actually there together they're going to learn far more from them than they are from me . . . they actually get security from being with somebody who is solid and kind of knows how it runs.

This built-up knowledge and experience from the older members of the choir was held in high regard and so the age limit within the choir rose over the years to accommodate those members who did not want to leave. Ann explained this was particularly relevant within the bass and tenor lines where replacements were hard to find.

Differences were noted between the established members and newcomers through age and experience. While Ann was categorically seen as the leader of the choir, an apprenticeship style of learning was commented on where the established members acted as choral leaders to new members. Monica stated, 'when you are first starting out, you look up to the established members' and Sam noted, 'the older members lead the group if the songs are new to newer members'. Parker also found amongst adolescent choral singers that, 'Through consistently singing with others, they became a team and then developed into leaders of the choral program. As leaders, they acted as social producers for others who were at the beginning their social identity process' (2014, p. 29).

At interview, members reiterated this established membership, peer support and roles played within an apprenticeship style of learning as seen in the extracts below:

there's leaders within the line.

(Joey)

there are people you can depend on.

(Karen)

we've [the basses] been here the longest so we're the most comfortable walking in, sitting down . . . because a lot of the music that we start we have done before.

(Chris)

Kristen in particular revealed a preoccupation for respecting the diverse nature of the choir members:

Everyone is different you know like all coming from different aspects of music and people are at different levels and you can learn a lot from the different people in the choir . . . everyone's kind of got different strengths and weaknesses so I think you pick up a lot from everybody in the choir.

In this way, she felt that all members, whether established or new, brought something different to the group.

Local government was seen as a critical stakeholder to the CLYC and key to fostering a sense of 'belonging' to the community. The CLYC case was a particularly leading example of a musical community that enjoys much local government support and a strong affiliated identity. The members spoke in glowing terms about this support and felt that the choir's existence relied heavily on such input. Many of the members commented on the strong reputation it brought with it. Joey, for instance, claimed, 'it brings a sense of pride to it, we kind of represent Limerick youth' and Chris echoed, 'it is a good name to have'. What was most interesting were the comments on the human side of the policy-makers' involvement. Joey commented:

> when we see Jill [the arts officer], we're happy to see her. She asks us how we are and she says thank you to each individual person as they leave so it's really sort of a support emotionally as well, that she cares and you feel that off her.

This had strong echoes with Ann's emphasis on the importance of relationship-building over time, where she stated, 'I think she [the arts officer] genuinely let me kind of take the reins, once she knew that I was capable of doing it, which was fair enough she had to sound me out'.

Just as relationship-building was important between the choir and local government arts office, so too was relationship-building within the choir. The focus group interview revealed in strong terms the significant leadership role played by choral director Ann. As with the participant log findings, the members spoke in glowing terms about Ann's musical expertise but equally about her nurturing nature as choral director. Marianne related:

> I've learned incredible amounts from her so like musically she is the best and then her actual personality . . . she knows when you can joke and she knows when to make us take it seriously but she is never ever like a teacher, she's still very caring, almost like a parent.

This feeling of a close-knit 'family' with Ann viewed in a semi-parental role (and in the case of one member as an actual parent) emphasised the significance of strong bonds, close relationships and 'belonging' that arose within membership in the CLYC.

When asked about affordances to the success of the CLYC, the focus group had only one response – their choral director. They spoke in emphatic terms about her leadership, and as before pointed out her dual role as musical expert and nurturer to the group. Most of them felt that their loyalty and commitment to the choir stemmed from Ann's leadership. Karen commented, 'she [Ann] makes everything happen, she's the reason we come, she's the person that makes us happy when we're here, she's the person that makes us work, she makes it so enjoyable'.

Factors that impinged on the enjoyment of the choir were mutually related in that they were cited as absenteeism and time-constraints. In this way, lack of participation and barriers to fostering 'belonging' significantly impacted on their sense of non-enjoyment. Members were 'frustrated', 'upset' and 'annoyed' when others did not turn up for rehearsal and worried about the pressure it caused for the choral director. Joey commented, 'I could see Ann was stressed'. They essentially did not enjoy this shirking of group responsibility which was usually a strong element of the choir's identity.

In brief, the CLYC formed and projected a distinctive practice of 'belonging' that was characterised through its identity as a local government initiative, but also the socio-musical interactions which formed a collective sense of 'belonging' amongst the group where familial comparisons were common. The distinctive 'belonging' practices of the choir can be characterised then as: valuing a caring leadership approach, prizing a local government identity, building socio-musical relationships over time, and learning through actual membership and peer support.

Summary

From the triangulation of four distinct data sets, taking account of both group and individual perspectives, significant practices in relation to the CLYC case study emerged. First, the choir maintained a goal-orientated focus throughout the rehearsals and performances which manifested as an interplay of leadership and group responsibility. There was also a goal-orientated emphasis on performance throughout the music-making.

The musical and social interactions were very much integrated where close-knit relationships were promoted and roles defined through seniority. Learning occurred through the choir's use of musical signifiers, gestures and cues, through the leadership of the choral director and group input, as well as self and group evaluation. Strong musical identities were projected which overlapped with multiple music communities. 'Belonging' emerged as a distinctive practice within the choir.

The choir represented a distinctive CoMP from the 'real world' which had strong links with local government. Through multiple data sets, the study provided an example from the youth and choral sector of how such musical communities learn, interact, form identities and build relationships.

5   An online community

Paul: Just wanted to let you know how much these lessons are improving my technique. Although i've been playing wooden flute for two years i still consider myself a beginner . . . and without realising it, i was developing some bad habits. Seems like i was spending as much time trying to figure out how to interpret ornamentation from books and write down the 'notes' as i was actually playing them!? Since finding you guys, i have stopped writing everything down and instead, will just watch you play slowly through a tune. This has REALLY freed me up . . . guess i was making things harder than they had to be. Its actually fun to practice now. The more i practice, the more fun it is, and the more fun it is the more i play. HaHa.

The above extract taken from the Online Academy of Irish Music (OAIM) chat forum highlights the importance of visual learning to members' musical practices. Implicit as well as explicit visual cues taken from the OAIM video tutorials are acknowledged here. This strong discourse, tradition and culture of Irish traditional music transmission was continually reinforced through the OAIM encouraging oral and aural learning. Furthermore, the posting of this learner's progress on a chat forum underlined the community practices of sharing experiences of playing and practising music that were a feature of this online community of musical practice (CoMP).

This chapter extends the medium of CoMP to a relatively new and emerging form of musical participation; an online musical community.[1] The OAIM is examined here to uncover community, musical and distinctive practices as with the previous two illustrations. Findings on both community and musical practices are set out. Particular to this case, tradition emerges as a distinctive practice and this is discussed in-depth. Each set of practices are evidenced from both group and individual perspectives. Due to the online nature of the case, observations of group perspectives include: the website, online forums, a 'cybersession', Facebook page and video tutorials. Interviews and participant logs illuminate individual insights.

---

1 Parts of this chapter appear in Kenny, A. (2013) 'The next level': investigating teaching and learning within an Irish traditional music online community. *Research Studies in Music Education* 35(2) 234–248.

As a third illustration of CoMP, qualitative data was gathered over a nine-month fieldwork period to uncover the practices (or *modus operandi*) of the OAIM as with the previous two cases.

The OAIM was set up in September 2010 and so provided the research with a perspective on an emerging CoMP. The site involves an 'e-learning system' where the tutorials combine video, audio, manuscript, text and optional feedback. It claims that 'When you join OAIM, you are joining a community of Irish music learners and lovers from all over the world who share one thing in common – they want to be better musicians' (www.oaim.ie). It is a subscription site where 'basic membership' can be gained for free to browse the site with limited access to sample lessons ('tasters' of the video tutorials). A full access subscription[2] incurs monthly fees, which gives unrestricted access to the website and its resources.

The site offers 42 separate courses through video tutorials available across 15 Irish traditional instruments. The tutors are highly reputable musicians and educators of national and sometimes international acclaim in Irish traditional music circles. The OAIM also has chat forums for subscribers, monthly e-shot newsletters for basic members and subscribers, as well as a Facebook page with open access. By the end of the data fieldwork period (June 2011), the highest percentage of both members and paid subscribers were from the United States of America (USA) at 35%. Ireland and the United Kingdom had roughly the same amount of subscribers (at 20 and 19% respectively). These were by far the most significantly represented countries with Germany, Canada, Australia, France and Spain accounting for another 20% cumulatively. Other countries that featured (though at only 1% coverage) spanned to such far-reaching countries as Brazil, Martinique and Japan. The age ranges of the members and subscribers predominantly (61%) lay within the 45 to 64 age bracket. This was interesting considering worldwide, over half of Internet users are under the age of 34 (www.statista.com), but also corresponds with a narrowing of a generation gap in relation to the same in recent years (Lenhart, Purcell, Smith, & Zickuhr, 2010). As well as this, it corresponded to data on musical pathways and life histories, where sometimes people learn new instruments or new genres late in life, or return to an instrument after a considerable time period has lapsed (Lamont, 2011; Pitts, 2012).

Community practices

Community practices which were interactional, communicative and performance-based were examined in-depth. To gain a holistic account of the online case, data findings from group discourse were therefore crucial. Interviews with three of the tutors (one of whom was also the co-founder) as well as eight members' participant logs served to gather individual perspectives into the OAIM community practices and support the broader analysis of the case.

---

2 A monthly subscription was €19.95.

Group perspectives

Relationships, membership, identity formation and collective knowledge-building through social networking led to an emergence of community practices within a shared online space. The 'classroom chat forum' was a user discussion forum on the OAIM website open to subscribers and tutors. The OAIM Facebook[3] page grew within the fieldwork period from 257 'friends' in October 2010 to over 1,000 by June 2011. This also meant increased posts, interaction and comments over time. The online forums particularly provided a window into members' community practices through their interactions with each other.

Forum users' online names and avatars (a visual representation of the user such as an image, photograph etc.) revealed much about identity formation and projection in the online community. Identity formation as a community practice was often evident in the chat forums with information about where members were from, why they were subscribing, practising habits, careers and previous related experiences of Irish traditional music. Below, we see 'psychodonald' sharing such information on the chat forum and explaining his choice of online name:

> *'psychodonald'*: Hi, just signed up for lessons. I'm a beginning flute student; however, I play other instruments, Bohem Flute, Bagpipes for quite a while. It has been difficult to impossible to locate an Irish Flute tutor in Salt Lake City, Utah. With a population as large as this city has, one would think there would be someone out there, but to no avail. I'm very fortunate, in my opinion, to have found the OAIM site and I'm looking forward to the lessons. BTW,[4] don't be alarmed by the 'psychodonald,' I'm a mental health, substance abuse professional therapist, plus law enforcement officer and began using the 'psychodonald' name as I thought it was quite clever at the time. Turns out, not so much. ☺ You know, 'psycho = psychology' 'donald = my first name,' hence 'psychodonald.' Oh well, live and learn, I guess. Do to my newness with the simple flute system, I'm looking forward to the lessons from Kate as I understand she handles the less experienced students. Kate, you noted that you always have tea with you, with me it's Coke Zero. I doubt you have that product in Ireland, you might be better off. At any rate, nice to be receiving the lessons.

Here, we see 'psychodonald' creating an identity on the chat forums that is humorous and open, depicted through making fun of his online name, the use of an emoticon[5] and associating himself with a beverage. We also see geographical barriers to accessing Irish traditional music in Utah, USA. Although not a career

---

3 Facebook (www.facebook.com) is a social networking Internet site. Since its launch in 2004 it now boasts over 1.35 billion active users worldwide.

4 BTW is an abbreviation for 'by the way'.

5 An emoticon uses punctuation, letters or cartoon images to form a facial expression or mood pictorially, e.g. ☺ (happy) and ☺ (wink).

for him, 'psychodonald' projected a strong music-related identity in listing off his previous instrumental experience as well as being explicit about his beginner status on the flute.

The use of avatars also revealed interesting insights in relation to the members' identity formation within their community practices. The avatars often depicted the members playing instruments or a pictorial/cartoon image of an instrument alone. One member for example, Irvine, presented a musical identity with the fiddle he held in his avatar. Irvine was not smiling in the picture which may also reveal to the viewer a 'seriousness' to this member's identity as a musician. Also in the shot were several other stringed instruments on stands, where Irvine was projecting a multi-instrumentalist identity.

Across the topics and threads in the chat forums, interactional practices of the users through the types of questions and comments could be broken down and summarised into the following categories: clarification, requests, progression updates, relating experiences, knowledge sharing and feedback. Despite the often-assumed solitary nature of learning from the Internet, much of the learning was carried out and/or related in a collective manner through the chat forums. For example, we see learners self-assessing their progress, 'I can land on the G about half the time without thinking about it' (Quickfiddler), accessing expertise from tutors as they need it, 'would it be best to master these rudiments before trying to use them?' (Paul), applying knowledge gained through e-learning tools, 'listening to the mp3 helped reprogram my fingers' (Quickfiddler) and feeding back on their learning 'a few things have fallen into place this past ten days' (Irvine). Hence, the chat forums emphasised both individual and group learning through a reflection process of sharing within the OAIM. Tutors too shared knowledge and experiences, hence facilitating online dialogue, as seen in the examples here:

> as far as finding a more serious bodhrán is concerned. I'd nearly advise waiting to actually try one from a maker you like or at least order one from a maker who's drums you've heard live? By the way, they all sound awful for the first year!
>
> (Ben)

> I'm not sure if you are in N. America, but something I have noticed from my time over there is that there are so many kiddie friendly folk festivals with children's performers and child friendly environments. I would love to organise something like that over here – most of the traditional music happens in the pubs.
>
> (Kate)

Here, without the confines of teaching to a structured lesson on a video tutorial, the tutors' style is much more casual, conversational and intimate. Personal anecdotes, connections and details fed into an emerging development of 'shared repertoire' among a 'community of learners' here which included the tutors.

Experiences of learning through the OAIM were also related on the Facebook page (akin to the chat forums):

Martin: Awesome Place and site . . . love it
OAIM: Glad you are enjoying it! We are constantly developing the site – thanks for the encouraging feedback.
Martin: Accessibility is a great gift and more with awesome Artists in there giving time and energy . . . Go raibh maith agat . . . Le meas [translation from Irish: 'Thank you . . . regards/with respect']

Here Martin was expanding the audience from the classroom chat forum to share his positive experience with the OAIM on Facebook. The OAIM encouraged feedback and marked their appreciation. Martin also recognised the issue of access and then the OAIM acting as a source to open up Irish traditional music learning opportunities through the Internet. We also see a reference to the Irish language here which was a common community practice throughout the Facebook posts and chat forums. This resonated with the overall interest in Ireland, Irish traditional music and a sense of the 'local', fostered by the OAIM through routine posts and images on Facebook (this is discussed in more detail later).

Although not physically face-to-face, relationships within the OAIM were formed via cyberspace – connecting with human beings as opposed to inanimate learning resources. In the following excerpt we see a specific example of an interaction between one learner (Irvine) and tutor (Kate) from the forum:

Irvine: Hi there Monica and all, just introducing myself – I joined a few days ago after having been pointed in this direction by the good folk on The Session. I have been playing mandolin for a good while, so I hope that this will be of some use when making the switch to the fiddle. So far, it seems to be helping – fingering obviously, but even the plectrum practice is making the bowing reasonably intuitive – and of course there's plenty of tunes in my nod! . . . Thanks for making the lessons so clear Monica, though I am puzzled how you can see what I am doing because you keep saying 'good'! Looking forward to sharing tips and chat from time to time.
Kate: Hi Irvine, glad to hear you are enjoying Monica's lessons. How are you finding the switch from mandolin to the fiddle? I am a flute player, however I would love to learn bouzouki and am going to try and find the time to do Brendan's course 'Bouzouki Basics'. As a melody player, the world of chords is intriguing to say the least. It's just finding the time needed to devote to a new instrument.

The exchange indicated an attempt at connecting, fashioning of identities, building relationships and community practices through the forum. Irvine has been directed to the OAIM through participation in another online Irish traditional community – the Session,[6] marking a distinct commitment to Irish traditional music. There was a shared understanding made between tutor and learner here in starting new challenges due to a love of musical learning within this interaction, thus projecting strong music-related identities. This exchange resonates with Turino's writings, 'in realising our own identities, we tend to foreground aspects that are regarded as important by the people around us' (Turino, 2008, p. 102).

Additionally, Irvine joked about online tuition in this post which was indicative of the type of 'in-joke' within the interactions on the OAIM forums. The online nature of the teaching and learning was often commented on and joked about in the chat forums. For example, Dan jested:

> I must say that I really do appreciate Tim's patience with me on this. No matter how many times I ask him to replay a section, he's unfailingly cheerful and ends by saying, 'brilliant' even if I completely flub the melody. Such is the magic of eLearning.

'In-jokes' are a regular feature of cultivating a community of practice (CoP) according to Wenger, signifying the emergence of a 'shared repertoire' between participants (Wenger, 1998). These jokes about e-learning became a regular feature of interactions on the forums. According to Ewing, this indicates a building of 'community' and shared culture of practice (2008, p. 581) where using jokes 'is a way for new members to show they understand the culture'.

A sense of 'mutual accountability' (Wenger, 1998) was often present in the chat forums too. For instance, Paul related, 'I managed to play a duet with our piper this week without letting the side down! Still a lot of work to do on tone, precision etc. but it's coming on well for only one month in'. Here a sense of group responsibility to the OAIM was evident even though the activity was outside of the online realm. This mutual accountability was often facilitated and fostered by the tutors, as seen in the chat forum posts below:

> *Kate*:   If any of you have requests for tunes you would like me to teach in my next course – let me know. I can't promise that I will include them – it depends on their appropriateness for the techniques I'll be covering
>
> *Tommy*: McFadden's handsome Daughter ☺
>
> *John*:   thanks for this nice offer Kate, my request would be for you to teach a tune you really like that hasn't been recorded commercially, or that has not been recorded very much or for a long time – that would be really cool and special
>
> *Fiona*:   There are a couple of tunes I'm learning from sheet music: 'The Ashplant' and 'The Old Woman in the Glen'; I don't know if they

---

6 www.thesession.org is an open membership website for the exchange of Irish traditional music tunes, events, sessions and recordings.

are suitable for the course. Then I'm also learning on the flute (transposed into D) a Scottish tune (a set actually) as played by The Tannahill Weavers: 'Roddie MacDonald's Favourite'. Cheers!

Kate: So, I have just set up the microphone and the video camera – any last minute suggestions? I'll be doing McFadden's Handsome Daughter, The Ashplant and a couple of lesser known ones for John. Here goes! ☺

In seeking guidance and collaborative input here, Kate fostered a sense of shared ownership over the decision-making in the OAIM. In this way, there was a building of shared learning evident in this extract where the learners linked back to previous knowledge and experience to influence this collaborative knowledge-building. Kate created a very open manner casually, taking on suggestions and keeping members informed of her decisions and actions. Also, there was a feeling of excitement and involvement in Kate's final 'here it goes', thereby instilling a sense of 'togetherness' in the upcoming course despite the fact that she was recording the video tutorials alone, in front of a video camera.

Individual perspectives

The OAIM website began from personal motivations. Kate, the coordinator, related at interview that it was born from 'a desire to make a living, live rurally and work from home'. Expectations were mismatched with reality, Kate admitted. The time, input and workload of the OAIM coupled with the gradual, slow nature of building the online community were underestimated. Access emerged as a major motivating factor to join the OAIM with members citing geographical barriers to tuition, and particularly high-quality tuition in Irish traditional music. For instance, Morris related, 'Since I do not live in Ireland and can only go to fiddle workshops in Ireland once or twice a year, I thought it was a good way of getting lessons' while Lorna wrote in her log, 'I have moved to Rio de Janeiro where I am devastated because there are no sessions, only one piper'. Members' expectations revolved around learning a new instrument, improving their playing and receiving tuition that was not to be found within easy reach. Extending this further, Andy was explicit in stating that the OAIM offered him 'structured instruction' that was missing on other Internet sites such as YouTube.

Due to the 'home-grown' nature of the OAIM, personal relationships with other Irish traditional musicians heavily shaped the OAIM tutor involvement but also the style of teaching that is both musical and social. These 'complementary contributions' (Wenger, 1998) draw upon multiple forms of competence to build a CoP as well as a sense of 'collaborative knowledge building' (Scardamalia & Bereiter, 1991). Kate relied heavily on the opinions and expertise from these tutors within a community of local Irish traditional musicians. Tim commented, 'I love just sitting down and having conversations, how it's working, not working, the direction it could take'. Kate remarked on the criticality of these personal relationships throughout the interview, 'that's been the advantage of having these friends, they just want it to work'. These relationships were also vital in sourcing tutors, where most of the tutors knew each other over a long period of time through Irish traditional music circles.

Born as a family lifestyle venture that relied on personal relationships, community practices were shaped through relationships both on and offline. This meant ongoing feedback and evaluation. With regard to the video tutorials, Tim noted, 'I was given free rein, there were no terms or conditions per se'. This trust, Ben believed, was a result of 'the choice of teachers . . . professionals who are at the cutting edge of their profession'. The tutors found that there was, in a sense, a forced reflection and evaluation of their teaching due to the online nature of the tuition. Tim shared:

> initially, in the first couple of modules I was incredibly self-conscious and I was listening to every word I was saying, I was looking at myself in terms of the eyes of the student, so I was really critical of myself, I kept going back and deleting classes . . . I had to deconstruct, had to think about how I have taught over the years and try to put a structure to that.

As the OAIM was leaving familiar face-to-face tuition territory for the tutors and coordinator, early feedback from members proved vital to tailoring the resource and shaping the community's practices. Specifically, Kate singled out one student who had a very direct impact on the OAIM:

> One in particular was an e-learning specialist, we chose to take it on board what he was saying and that was when we changed all our lessons into their current lesson templates. We started to devise more of a system and made it much more visual . . . it was worth it you know, it has really made it something, it's not just a video anymore.

Just as the community of musicians/tutors contributed to the start-up of OAIM, the community of learners contributed to its continued growth and development of practices (this was also evidenced earlier with Kate's call for tune requests).

The teacher and learner roles within the OAIM were clearly defined. The tutors saw themselves as professional teachers delivering quality online tuition. These notions of 'quality' and 'professional' status of the tutors were mentioned frequently during the interviews. Tim related, 'I knew this was uncharted territory, like there is a lot of music on the Internet, but, you know there are a lot of short courses or free youtube clips but there is not that much that has done something consistently . . . that's of really high quality'. Ben echoed this: 'I think people who do this particular course are assured of a very high standard of teacher'. The type of online teaching provided by the OAIM then was seen as distinct to other Internet sources due to its focus on high-quality teaching, scaffolded sequenced courses and calibre of tutors. The learners too noted the importance of this high-quality, professional approach. Matt commented in his log, 'I feel connected to a person who clearly knows what she is doing. The fact that she is so qualified to teach is really important to me'.

As an evolving initiative, Kate valued the importance of building community practices through long-term subscribers and developing relationships between tutors and learners. She believed this was achieved through the tutors' teaching approaches and a promotion of the student locating their own playing style and/or musical identity:

> we've been trying to mimic a one-on-one class so you feel like sitting there with your tutor and the way like amidst the repetition and the mimicry there's just room for talk on technique and style and encouraging the student to experiment with different things you know and develop their own style.

Here, Kate was also referring to the importance of the online forums to encourage relationship-building and 'room for talk' within the emerging CoMP.

Within the video tutorials, this attention to dialogue from the tutors was evident, despite teaching alone to a camera. Kate felt this was missing in other websites while Tim commented, 'I chat away to the camera saying that's great, that's great. They like the personality coming through, you know the bit of chat'. The style of the OAIM tutors, despite teaching to a camera, very much centred on a casual, dialogic approach. This dialogic practice on the video tutorials, as well as the online forum interactions, all served to foster a sense of community. Dialogue between the learners themselves was also encouraged through the chat forums to build a social network of practice online; however, all of the interviewees commented on the slow nature of this engagement to grow while recognising the need for time to build relationships.

The members, having only been subscribed for at most six months at that point, noted in the logs that they were all 'learners' with no change in this role over this short time period. The inclusive atmosphere within the OAIM was commented on in the logs frequently which was claimed to help foster relationships between members. Irvine writes, 'It meets a need and seems like a friendly place', while Alice wrote, 'The enthusiasm of others encourages me to keep at it'. Members related a heightened sense of enjoyment when they felt welcome, in 'a friendly place', included and essentially part of a learning community. This relationship-building between the learners and tutors as well as between the learners themselves occurred despite having never met face to face. For example, Andy revealed: 'Love starting one of Kate's videos. When the only instruction you've had is by book, a warm, engaging instructor is a vast improvement – makes me want to practise'. Here, the feeling of forming a relationship with the tutor was important not just to musical progression but also to an overall sense of belonging to the community. Tim commented at interview, 'It is trying to combine the lesson with feedback and the forums, trying to create that sense of community, of people coming together that YouTube clips mightn't have'.

In brief, the OAIM as an emerging CoMP was developing community practices throughout the fieldwork period. Salient evolving community practices were characterised then as the practices of: forming relationships through dialogical interactions, sharing experiences, learning and knowledge, projecting music-related identities, and collaborating through collective input on and offline.

Musical practices

The OAIM is an online community and learning resource for Irish traditional music. Therefore, participation in the CoMP centred on musical learning. Musical practices emerged through the e-learning systems and structures, members' online interactions as well as sharing a performance practice through a cybersession. Group and individual perspectives of these musical practices are presented here.

Group perspectives

The structure of the OAIM e-learning system was set up as a four-step pedagogical process: (1) online courses, (2) support materials, (3) chat forums, and (4) optional feedback. The video tutorials retained an Irish traditional music pedagogy through a consistent focus on aural and oral learning through repetition, albeit in a technologically mediated space. Other resources such as sheet music and mp3[7] listening files were offered as support materials as well as the discussion forums for subscribers and tutors. Subscribers had the option of gaining specific, private feedback by purchasing 'tokens' where they could upload a video or audio of their playing for comment from the tutor in either written or mp3 form.

The structure of each music course[8] contained 12 to 14 video tutorials which each lasted approximately 15–30 minutes. The tutors sat quite close to the video camera and talked, played and/or sang directly into it. Produced in each tutor's home, each course bore a distinctive background. The courses followed a sequence of development where technique, skills and style were scaffolded through tune playing. The repertoire spanned different Irish traditional modes from a hornpipe, jig, set dance, slow air and reel.[9] The pedagogy of the tutorials built up such aspects as ornamentation, variation, phrasing and articulation over the full course through actual repertoire/tunes. Veblen and Waldron explain (2008, p. 101):

> Irish instrumental music offers a most convenient and portable meme for transmission in emerging media. Each tune is a complete unit, a small and finite form that includes repetition and opportunities for variation within limits.

One video extract, taken from the course 'Flute Fundamentals', taught by tutor and co-founder Kate, demonstrated a typical example of a beginning to a lesson.

---

7 mp3 is a standard audio format for audio storage where the data is compressed for transfer and playback on digital audio recorders.
8 The OAIM courses offered during the fieldwork period were: Fiddle Basics, Fleadh Tunes for the Fiddle, Bouzouki Basics, Bodhrán Basics, Expert Whistle Skills, Expert Whistle Skills 2, Fleadh tunes for the Irish Flute, Traditional Irish Song (English Language), Intermediate Uilleann Pipes Technique, Flute Foundations, Flute Progressions, Concertina Skills, Piano Tunes and Accompaniment.
9 These modes or different types of Irish traditional tunes all have varying time signatures and specific features associated with them. All of the modes have accompanying dances in hard or soft shoes except for the slow air which is not traditionally danced to.

In this lesson Kate is playing and teaching the tune 'Fig for a Kiss'. The tune is played in full twice, first without ornamentation and then with it. Kate looked straight at the camera and her fingering on the flute was fully exposed to the subscriber. In her first playing of the tune, she remained quite rigid. With the second playing, with ornamentation, her body began to sway and move to the music, suggesting a freer form of playing that relied on personal interpretation. This musical practice of playing through the tune repeatedly was carried out by all of the tutors in their teaching.

In this manner, the video tutorials essentially copied the traditional musical practice and style of learning within Irish music which is often referred to as 'passing it on'; an aphorism used to describe its oral transmission. Thus, instrumental tuition was taught through tunes and songs phrase by phrase aurally. This is again revealed in the extract from video tutorial observational field notes below:

> *'Fiddle Basics', lesson nine, taught by Monica. The tune is a jig in 6/8 time with a feel of two beats in the bar. This was the second part of the lesson teaching the first part of the tune 'Rose in the Heather'. Monica played this first part of the tune slowly and then broke down the tune phrase by phrase adding in ornamentation, the focus here on 'rolls'. 'Rolls' are playing five quavers in the space of three quavers, played with one bow stroke, by flicking the fingers off the strings. The ornament was isolated and then added into the tune. Repetition was consistently encouraged verbally, 'let's try that again', and in the repeated playing on the video.*
>
> (OAIMFBV9[10])

Here, we see a strong focus on repetition and imitation, as is customary in the teaching of Irish traditional music. The learner is encouraged to 'try that again', despite the tutor not actually hearing the learner's practice. All of the tutors often engaged in discourses associated with face-to-face lessons, such as praising the learner after a phrase is practised or repeated, with comments such as 'well done', 'very good' and 'that was great' used frequently across all courses (on average 10 phrases of praise per lesson were recorded). In addition, the tutors played along in repetitions, thereby creating a (cyber) space for a musical practice of music-making together as opposed to in isolation (though in a physical and temporal sense, they were of course separate). This had interesting links to the notion of creating a 'space', as put forward by de Certeau (de Certeau, 1984), through engagement or participation within this online 'place' (see Chapter 1).

As an emerging CoMP, learning tools were shaped and built up collectively as needs arose. For example, the use of mp3 files and notation as supports to the video tutorials was born from feedback from the learners' requests. Despite the

---

10 OAIMFBV9 refers to Online Academy of Irish Music Fiddle Basics Video 9. All video tutorials are classified in this way, with the number indicating the sequence of the video tutorial within the specific course.

inclusion of notation as a support, however, the learning through oral transmission, though online, was very dominant in keeping in the traditional style and culture of the genre (as seen within community practices earlier). This was made apparent through comments on the chat forums. For example, Ray posted, 'When i happened to pause a video and noticed you didn't have "little circles" pressed into your finger tips from the tone holes (like i do) i loosened my grip on the flute'. This strong discourse and convention of Irish traditional music transmission was then negotiated into this new online space and became a shared practice within the OAIM.

The 'cybersession' provided the research with a focus on a shared musical performance practice. The OAIM live streamed[11] an Irish traditional music session to an Internet audience from a pub in Doolin, Co. Clare in April 2011, using a partnership with LiveTrad.[12] The session featured live performances of Irish traditional music by some of the course tutors as well as local musicians. The cybersession saw nine musicians sitting in a semi-circular fashion in a corner of the pub. The set-up and delivery of the cyber session very much captured a characteristic Irish traditional music pub session or musical performance practice. This was evident in the tunes that were played, the casual unrehearsed atmosphere, the old-style pub setting, the arrangement of the musicians in an inward-looking circle and the non-verbal gestures used between them such as eye contact, nods and foot tapping. As well as this, in the playing of the tunes there appeared to be few limits to the playing, with musicians coming in seemingly where they 'felt' it was time to play. This was especially noticeable at the beginning of the tunes with one or two musicians starting a tune with the other instruments joining in stages. This all occurred with much laughter shared between the musicians as they played.

The cybersession appeared to try to capture the essence of group music-making in the Irish traditional music genre that was unachievable in the OAIM website teaching and learning format. Through capturing this musical performance practice the OAIM were further creating access to this aspect of Irish traditional music that is so important to the genre's identity and tradition. It also created an additional learning tool of listening to live music for its members and beyond, as well as fashioning an opportunity 'to take part' to a degree over the Internet through comments as well as the potential to play along.

Individual perspectives

There was a strong sense within the interviews and logs of approaching and developing musical practices in Irish traditional music tuition in new ways through

11 Live streaming is a method of broadcasting live over the Internet which usually involves a content delivery network to distribute and deliver the content as it is recording.
12 LiveTrad (www.livetrad.com) is a website dedicated to the live web streaming of Irish traditional music sessions, concerts and festival events. It is part funded through the Irish Arts Council and tourism agencies as well as corporate sponsors.

online learning. The tutors were excited about exploring an online environment as a new approach to teaching and learning. Kate commented:

> you get to a point in life where you know what you're good at. Particularly I love teaching music one on one, it's what I've had the pleasure of doing over the past 10 years . . . now it's just really bringing it to the next level.

There was an exploratory or experimental feeling to all of this, as Kate claims, departing from 10 years of experience in face-to face tuition. Tim echoed this, stating, 'I'd just be interested in new directions that tuition could take in Irish music, I'd always be thinking about what could happen online'. For Ben, he was keen to reiterate the value of 'the local' and high teaching standards regardless of the medium (live or in cyberspace). There were challenges associated with online teaching expressed by the tutors too, mainly in the 'strangeness' of lack of direct personal interaction when teaching to a video camera, but also regular frustration at not being able to sort out simple issues such as finger positioning instantly. Tim remarked, 'I just had to realise that if you teach something and you repeat it three or four times, that you don't have to do that – that you can rewind! That's strange because I just had to change the flow of it'.

Due to this new style of musical practice in teaching, the tutors felt that more preparation and structure were required with the online tutorials than with face-to-face tuition to 'change the flow if it'. These tutors (notably all under the age of 40) were clearly choosing to teach Irish traditional music in this technologically mediated way to explore new approaches to teaching and learning but also were mindful of retaining a sense of 'authenticity' in this developing environment.

There was strong evidence of multiple and overlapping musical practices among the members. Tim, one of the tutors, commented:

> if someone is learning online they are still going to look for that contact with other musicians even if it's not going in for an hour and paying for it, they are still going to meet up and learn when they are playing with somebody else. So I think it will always be another way of learning, they'll learn in this context, and then go and learn in another context.

Interestingly, of the 11 participant log responses, every member was involved in other musical activities described as performing/composing and/or listening to music. It was evident that the learners themselves often saw the OAIM as an addition to previous knowledge, experiences and practices of Irish traditional music. This sometimes manifested in the evidence of returning to a lapsed instrument or a way into learning another instrument in the same genre, akin to findings from Pitts (2005, 2009, 2012) and Lamont (2011) (see Chapter 1). Almost half of the respondents spent over 10 hours a week engaged in musical activities and nobody spent less than two hours. This indicated strong musical identities among the subscribers. Nine members from the 11 log entries noted they were engaged in other Irish traditional musical practice. These types of activities ranged from lessons, to sessions, to bands, to folk camps, to visiting residential courses in Ireland. We see here a demonstration of participants being within a 'nexus of multi-membership' (Wenger, 1998), engaged in other Irish traditional music activities outside of the OAIM.

Practising habits for members varied from person to person yet similar musical practices were in evidence. These practices included the use of learning tools (such as notation and metronomes) and more specifically e-learning tools (such as software to slow a tune down as well as the OAIM video tutorials). For example, Lauren shared in her log, 'I usually practice at home or at work after work hours (office is empty then). I usually start by playing/recapping a few tunes I was learning. Sometimes playing along with CDs, as well as material from the OAIM website'. Alice wrote of engaging with multiple resources for practising which included the video tutorials, notation, books and specialised software. Here she was mixing technology with more traditional tools for learning:

> I listen to the videos and then play along with the sheet music. I have not tried by ear very much but I will. I practice in my apartment in NY in the living or dining room with the computer on. I then practice from many books. I have other material using 'Transcribe' which slows it down for me to play.

Throughout the logs, the dedication to self-directed musical practice routines was very evident. 'Psychodonald' in his response described a habitual norm of including a certain soft drink in practice routines; this 'brand' was also used to mark out his identity as seen earlier:

> In my music room. First I log on to OAIM, review the lesson, have a Coke Zero, play the lesson with the teacher. Have a Coke Zero. Move through the entire lesson with the teacher and play with her playing. Have a Coke Zero. Go to the bathroom since I've had about a gallon of Coke Zero.

Despite the solitary nature of online playing, 'Psychodonald' practises alongside the tutor in the videos, in a sense creating a sense of collective music-making, although unbound by time and space. Aside from a general disappointment that the forums were not busier, the influence of interaction on the online forums on musical practice was felt to be an extra support and provided an inclusive feeling of 'we're in this together' between members. Lauren shared, 'I get support, makes me feel better about my playing'.

Progression in playing also emerged as important to members' musical practice. For example, Grant indicated a new ease found in playing, 'I realized that I am picking up tunes faster, and some of the ornaments are starting to flow automatically' while Irvine commented, 'Good to find that the lessons I have so far done are well presented and clear, and that they helped me to make progress'. It was obvious across all log entries that this feeling of progression in learning was what motivated members to sustain their musical practice as well as feel a sense of achievement.

The OAIM represented an emerging approach to Irish traditional music teaching and learning that broadened access to a worldwide community. The most significant emerging musical practices of the OAIM can be characterised as: integrating pedagogies of e-learning and traditional approaches, retaining multiple and overlapping musical identities, privileging oral transmission, and maintaining collective music-making and performance-based traditions.

Distinctive practice: tradition

The OAIM was rooted in a specific tradition delineated by the genre and Irish 'context' (despite being an online community). These tradition practices manifested themselves through the community and musical practices with particular reference to pedagogical and performance practices, projected ideology and identity as well as collective interactions. In this way, the practice of upholding tradition was a distinctive practice within this third illustration of CoMP (for a more detailed treatment of how national identity functioned within the OAIM, see Kenny, 2013a).

Group perspectives

The group data findings offered considerable insights into the OAIM sense of 'place' and due to the nature of the musical genre, collective feelings of Irish 'nationhood' which had interesting links with Benedict Anderson's notion of 'imagined' communities and 'nation-ness' discussed in Chapter 1 (Anderson, 1991). Taking these concepts as points of departure, tradition practices within the OAIM were formed via cyberspace, arguably an 'imagined space' with connections made through Irish traditional music. The theme of tradition continually revealed itself as significant in the case study data analysis where 'tradition' itself was referenced 37 times in the coding alone across 12 data sources.

The OAIM appeared to be bridging the worlds of Irish traditional music and new technology. The musical practices and pedagogical focus of the video tutorials encapsulated very strong genre-specific traditions. As discussed earlier, these practices were based on an emphasis on oral transmission, imitation and repetition, as is customary in learning Irish music. Tutorials scaffolded learning of skills such as ornamentation, variation, phrasing and articulation through actual tune playing. Attention to dialogue within the video tutorials as well as interacting on the online forums were seen as important by both the tutors and the learners. Thus, the musical and social processes were inter-related and drew from an Irish culture of dialogical practice.

The Facebook posts fostered an interest in the 'local' context of the OAIM and sense of attachment to a 'place' and tradition. Although a 'global' community on the Internet, the engagement with the OAIM here demonstrated a strong interest in the 'local' with multiple comments on the physical landscape and weather. One Facebook poster commented on a photo of Clare, 'This is my second and cultural home. It is just wild and very, very beautiful, just like the traditional music emanating from the very earth'. The location of the OAIM office in County Clare, Ireland then was seen as critical to its identity but also to its credentials to tutor Irish traditional music. This resonated with Marie McCarthy's writings where (1999, p. 189), 'The expanding sense of music as community has been paralleled by an equally powerful movement that refocuses music transmission in local communities'.

Genre-specific terminology and language used in the online forums also projected a tradition practice. References to well-known recordings, teachers and performers were prominent as evidenced in previous sections and in the following extract from the chat forum:

> *John*: I learned 'The Sporting Pitchfork' from an American whistle player and producer Bill Ochs, a really great guy. Do you know him? My all time favourite recorded version of this tune is the one Michael O Raghallaigh played on his CD 'Inside Out'.
>
> *Kate*: I don't know Bill Ochs – but I am familiar with Michael O Raghallaigh's playing – love it! . . . Just got back from Drumshanbo, Leitrim where there is a great festival – the area is full of great flute players. Was such a pleasure! Any good festivals in Palm Springs?

A sharing of knowledge as well as an attempt to make connections through known musicians and geographical 'places', even through such wide physical distances of Drumshanbo to Palm Springs, is evident here. In this way, there was an attempt to evoke tradition, through association with Irish traditional music performers and festivals.

This attachment or value given to tradition was further reinforced through the use of stories, anecdotes, memories and jokes – essentially Irish lore, relating directly to Ireland or a sense of 'Irishness' (O'Flynn, 2009). The following story related through the chat forum illustrated this projection of an Irish identity quite well where Barry shared a story about meeting his old Irish traditional music tutor 'out of context':

> His teaching came back to haunt him once – he was a border guard on the US side of the Canada US border and I was on the Canadian side. One day I was going across the border and as luck should have it Mr X was the guard. He had known me for years and when I drove up it was all by the book how many people in the car, what is the purpose of your trip. I answered in Gaelic and he told me English only. To no avail I wasn't going to budge – Gaelic only. Finally when he had finished questioning me he finally replied – Slán Anois [trans: bye, now] – I was the only person ever to get away with that. Everyone else – by the book. I do miss him and as he always used to say in a thick Philadelphia accent – god rest 'im.

Here, not only was there a great sense of nostalgia for the tutor but also for a connection felt to the deceased tutor through a sense of 'Irishness', clearly an identity shared through the traditional music and the Irish language. Phrases and salutations in the Irish language were often included in Facebook posts and chat forums which further rooted the OAIM in a specific, place-based tradition practice.

Stereotyped notions of Irish tradition were also prevalent and solely based on a rural image of Ireland. There were often assumptions made about complete immersion in Irish traditional music purely by being physically present in the country. For example, one subscriber wrote on the chat forum:

Paul: I live in rural Minnesota . . . far from a thriving Irish community and envy you who have grown up with this beautiful music! The picture of Kate enjoying a cup of tea while taking a walk speaks volumes.

Kate: Well, cups of tea are great for playing the flute; they keep the hands warm and relaxed and prevent injury. I am not sure what the temperature is like in Minnesota, but it can be chilly (especially indoors) in Ireland and I won't practice without a cuppa!

Here, a 'cup of tea' was referenced as it was used on the tutor's biographical information page on the website (thereby promoting such an 'Irish' connection) and picked up on as a stereotyped traditional image of Ireland. Furthermore, such stereotyped comments are verified by the tutor who goes further to comment on the weather. However, the notion that all Irish people grow up with Irish traditional music in a 'thriving Irish community' is an 'imagined' concept and equally ironic considering Kate is not actually from Ireland.

The OAIM Facebook page was characterised by many posts on the locality, images of Clare, jokes about Ireland, the weather and so on as well as posting many links to Irish traditional music events, festivals, courses and 'latest news' in the field. The text below shows some sample comments posted in response to a photographic image of the coastline in west Clare (where the OAIM office is based):

Garry: That's simply beautiful.
Marie: So green and beautiful
Dolores: WOW – Iontach ar fad [trans.: 'Wonderful all together']

The OAIM were projecting a very distinct tradition practice here through a physical and geographical identity despite existing in cyberspace. As well as this, we again see the use of the Irish language alongside the association with Ireland as 'green'. This connection and physical location of the OAIM office in County Clare emerged as critical to its Facebook and website identity.

During the cybersession, which of course encapsulated a tradition practice (see musical practices discussed earlier), an Internet audience of thousands who watched had the opportunity to input onto a common message board. The messages appeared online for all to view during the session but also many were read out by the musicians in the pub. The comments therefore connected the physical Irish pub setting with the world through the medium of cyberspace. The comments posted predominantly referenced Irish traditional music session memories, anecdotes and jokes, as well as nostalgic comments from Irish people living abroad as seen below:

Veronica: I'm so happy to listen to you all!! I'm from Argentina, far away but so near!!

Colm: Sounds great here too. Seeing the table made from the Singer sewing machine reminds me of Mother Redcap's Tavern back in the day. Seriously good sound though. Fair play indeed!

Suzanne: The live streaming of your session is brilliant! I want to crawl into the computer and join you!

From these comments, several features of 'connecting' with a tradition and performance practice, both through Irish traditional music and Ireland, were illuminated. Veronica punctuated the function of such an online resource as 'far away, but so near', while Suzanne wanted 'to crawl into the computer' to join. Colm directly related to old memories of Ireland sparked by a piece of furniture in the session. The comment 'fair play' also captured Irish slang for 'well done', further signifying an Irish identity focus to the cybersession.

Individual perspectives

A 'deep attachment' with Irish 'nation-ness' or tradition as a 'cultural artefact' (Anderson, 1991) within the OAIM was also very significant in the interviews and participant logs. For instance, Irvine states:

I like the idea that the lessons are from Ireland, where else would one go to ITM [Irish traditional music]? I know that there are many people who can teach ITM who don't live in Ireland; however, I just like the idea that my lessons come from Ireland. It's a very subjective and personal thing that currently defies the ability to explain.

Irvine here directly pointed to the 'imagined' nature of this connection – 'defies the ability to explain' – which resonates with Anderson's (1991) writings on nationalism where people can portray 'profound emotional legitimacy' to an 'imagined community'.

In being an online academy of Irish music, the OAIM had been mindful of encompassing tradition practice as Kate remarked on the use of traditional methods of teaching, 'We've very much kept the traditional techniques or methods of teaching Irish music, you know repetition and mimicry, we're repeating phrases again and again. There're a lot of tutorials on the Internet where there has been no discourse from the tutors'. Preserving the nature of teaching Irish traditional music with such techniques as 'repetition and mimicry' was all-important to the coordinator despite the medium of transmission being online. An attention to dialogue between playing from the tutors was also viewed as essential, which was deemed as missing from other websites (as discussed in an earlier discussion on community practices).

A connection to Ireland and a tradition practice was a significant source of enjoyment within this online community. As seen earlier, Irvine noted that he liked 'the idea that my lessons come from Ireland' while Zara wrote in her log, 'Taking the lessons is helpful and instructive in context of greater traditional canon'. It also emerged in the logs that many of the participants engaged in some element of performance connected to Ireland or 'Irishness'. These ranged from occasional social occasions to regular Irish traditional music sessions. These performances appeared to link directly with a sense of tradition/genre and the playing was an extension of that. For instance, Morris related that he played at social events such as birthdays of his 'Irish friends' whom he related are 'active in Irish Dancing'.

The cybersession also saw a direct link to tradition through performance practice where a 'typical' Irish traditional music pub session was streamed live (discussed earlier). This approach also served a need for Kate as co-founder of the OAIM to alleviate some local musicians' scepticisms about learning Irish traditional music online. This tension between the old and the new in Irish traditional music circles was made apparent during the interviews. Kate related:

> for a long time I was too embarrassed to tell them about it, I'd be out playing sessions and stuff with these local musicians and often I'd sit and listen to the conversation and they're so anti-internet and this, that and the other and I'd sit there just nodding my head, you know yourself, and now you know the cat's jumped out of the bag and they all know it's me! . . . it's a whole big juxtaposition like traditional music with a sort of earthy sort of sociability with it and the Internet which is so technical and you know cutting edge and advanced.

There appeared to be an identity struggle here that went beyond the OAIM between the Irish traditional music world remaining 'authentic' within a distinct tradition practice and embracing new technologies. Within this genre-specific CoMP then, the connection to Ireland and a 'local place' was imperative for the OAIM to retain and project as part of its developing identity online.

The tutors, when questioned about the 'authenticity' of delivering Irish traditional music tuition through an online medium, quickly dismissed such ideas. Tim shared:

> it is not better or worse, it's just different . . . in the same way that how I learned the pipes from my primary teacher, going up to his house every Monday evening, is different to going into a group and learning with 10 others, is different to not having any lessons at all and learning as you go along, so I think it is just different.

Ben also felt the OAIM represented a different context and way to learn music, stating, 'the student self selects to enrol and controls their own pace, but they are also selecting a teacher and their process and trusting and investing in that process. I think it's an excellent starting point for learning, compared to say "my parents made me do piano"'.

Preserving the tradition within the global phenomenon of cyberspace was clearly important to the OAIM. In summary, a distinctive practice of tradition was characterised by projecting a 'local' and 'Irish' identity, maintaining genre-specific traditions and teaching approaches, and fostering attachment through images, language and stories.

Summary

The group and individual perspectives gathered from across the multiple data sets revealed significant practices in relation to the OAIM as an emerging CoMP. The OAIM community practices manifested as dependent on relationships both on and offline where there was collaborative input into developing the community through a sharing of experiences, learning, knowledge and expertise. Members also projected strong music-related identities. With regard to musical practices, pedagogies engaged with integrated both e-learning and traditional approaches where there was a distinct emphasis on oral transmission, collective music-making and performance-based traditions. Retaining multiple and overlapping musical identities was also part of this community's practices. Tradition emerged as a distinctive practice within the OAIM where a 'local' and 'Irish' identity was fashioned and projected. Maintaining genre-specific traditions, teaching approaches as well as fostering attachment to tradition through images, language and stories all characterised this distinctive practice.

This third illustration of a CoMP aimed to provide an important 'window' into how one online musical community developed and sustained musical, community and distinctive practices. In this way, the OAIM case study triangulates with the other two cases of the jazz ensemble (Chapter 3) and youth choir (Chapter 4), in examining important issues within a sociocultural theory of learning. The online setting for this musical community extends the medium of 'musical worlds' and the development of a CoMP to a continually emerging form of musical participation.

Part III

Insights from communities of musical practice

6 Understanding communities of musical practice

This chapter presents a discussion across all three communities of musical practice (CoMPs) examined: the jazz, choral and online communities. Significant relationships, issues and themes across all cases are explored to draw together insights into the development of musical communities more broadly. According to Becker, 'Studying society is a process of back and forth, looking in the world, thinking about what you've seen, and going back to have another look at the world' (1998, p. 146). Using a community of practice (CoP) framework as a lens, this cross-case comparison draws from data findings holistically to make explicit the links, commonalities and differences between the 'musical worlds' investigated. A sense of belonging, collaborative learning and identity-building emerged as key to each community's development and sustainability. This reveals the importance of a sociocultural learning system within musical communities and sheds light on contemporary debates about how, why and where people learn music together.

Revisiting the community of practice framework

The CoP framework (Lave & Wenger, 1991; Wenger, 1998, 2006; Wenger, et al., 2002; Wenger & Snyder, 2000) employed within this cross-case comparison took the social process of learning within musical communities as its focus. As described in Chapter 2, the CoMPs studied were identified based on an assumption that the three dimensions of 'mutual engagement', 'joint enterprise' and 'shared repertoire' were present (Lave & Wenger, 1991; Wenger, 1998). In addition, Wenger's (1998, p. 125) set of 14 indicators that form a CoP were used to identify the development of a CoP within the three case studies which included such aspects as: 'shared ways of engaging', 'knowing what others know, what they can do, and how they can contribute to an enterprise', 'local lore, shared stories, inside jokes' and 'rapid flow of information and propagation of innovation'.

Encapsulating Bourdieuian (1977; 1979; 1984; 1990; 2002) theory as well as the sociocultural theories of Vygotsky (1962; 1978; 1993), Bruner (1996) and Lave and Wenger (1991) (discussed in Chapter 1), how the experience of learning, meaning-making and identity connected within a 'social learning system' (Wenger, 2006) to build a CoMP within three distinct contexts is of significant

Table 6.1 Wenger's dimensions of CoP (1998) and areas of focus for cross-case comparison

Dimensions of CoP	Description	Areas of focus
Mutual engagement (domain)	The actual *domain*, the regular interaction and sets of relationships that form a common endeavour.	Participation Membership Relationships
Joint enterprise (process)	The *process* itself and the interactions, shared goals and negotiation that it entails.	Negotiated enterprise Indigenous enterprise Mutual accountability
Shared repertoire (practice)	The actual *practice*, ways of doing, joint pursuit and shared resources that are used to make and negotiate meaning.	Jokes and laughter Lore Learning tools

importance. The use of the CoP framework for analysis builds on the work of other studies discussed throughout the book to expand its use to broader contexts, genres and mediums. The CoP framework is thus employed as both an analytical and interpretative tool for this cross-case comparison.

The triumvirate of the CoP model of mutual engagement, joint enterprise and shared repertoire as well as the 14 indicators of a CoP (Wenger, 1998, pp. 125–6) manifested themselves consistently throughout the three cases. Key characteristics of community, musical and distinctive practices from each CoMP (outlined in Chapters 3, 4 and 5) also underpinned and interrelated with the three dimensions of CoP. Thus, the data findings across multiple data sets from each individual case chapter expand and draw new insights under the CoP framework. In this way, the CoP dimensions act as a broad analytical framework, or as 'thinking tools' (Burnard, 2012b) for this discussion. Table 6.1 (adapted from Table 1.1, Chapter 1) serves as a useful reminder of how the three dimensions of the CoP framework guided the thematic cross-case comparison.

The study, underpinned by this sociocultural framework, took a situated perspective of the CoMPs examined. In other words, the comparison did not seek to assume any assumptions or trends across all three cases as each community was viewed as distinctive. Rather, this chapter offers a means to situate the study within a broader conceptual framework to seek deep understandings of how CoMPs develop and sustain themselves. Through such a framing and use of data findings to punctuate the analysis, it is hoped that this chapter can offer important insights into sustainable CoMP models within policy and practice.

Mutual engagement

There was a clear *modus operandi* within the three CoMPs studied which could be viewed as the 'habitus' (Bourdieu, 1977, 1984, 1990; Bourdieu & Johnson, 1993) or shared ways of doing things distinct to each musical community. For example, both the County Limerick Youth Choir (CLYC) and Limerick Jazz Workshop (LJW) had their respective practices of beginning and ending rehearsals just as the Online Academy of Irish Music (OAIM) had common structures within the video tutorials and social media mechanisms. Within such a 'situated learning' (Lave & Wenger, 1991) viewpoint, participation, membership and relationships are discussed.

Participation

'Legitimate peripheral participation' is a salient concept within the CoP framework where boundaries are unclear within community participation and occur at multiple levels (Lave & Wenger, 1991; Wenger, 1998). Key to such participation is access to the CoP and its learning resources. These learning resources could be described as information, knowledge and tools. Learning through participation interrelated with issues of identity-building where, as Wenger explains, 'learning is an experience of identity' (1998, p. 215) in so far as knowledge forms (and informs) identity.

Group music-making was of course what formed the basis for mutual engagement within the CLYC and LJW and thus defined the members' participation levels as well as motivation to join the two communities. For example, Sam from the CLYC commented, 'I expected to feel like part of the group and was looking forward to singing with others' while a member of the LJW noted, 'I had to really practise playing with other people . . . to play with a band' (Leona). Learning then for these groups occurred to a large degree through participation or 'collaborative knowledge building' (Scardamalia & Bereiter, 1991, 1996). This was evident within the video observations too, where, for instance, the members of the LJW were observed running through small passages in twos or threes, engaging in non-verbal cues during playing and becoming much more creative with their playing in response to each other (see Chapter 3). This collaborative learning occurred therefore as a result of participation in both musical and community practices.

The issue of access was most pronounced within the OAIM, due to its very nature as an online community. It was very apparent that members felt that the OAIM was serving specific learning needs and facilitating a collaborative learning environment to provide Irish traditional music tuition to geographical areas with no or limited access to tuition in this genre (see Chapter 5). This focus on self-directed learning and motivation to join the OAIM drew parallels with Wenger's concept of 'individual learning trajectories' (Wenger, 2006) where Wenger emphasised a shift in learning from formal education to 'communities of practice', thereby giving participants more agency in their learning through participation. This was also echoed frequently on the chat forums, where, for example, 'psychodonald' posted:

> It has been difficult to impossible to locate an Irish Flute tutor in Salt Lake City, Utah. With a population as large as this city has, one would think there would be someone out there, but to no avail.

It became clear, however, within the OAIM case study that access was not just a geographical concern but also one caught up in the notion of identity-building through mutual engagement. This was evident most prominently in the inter-actional practices of the OAIM. For example, on the online forum, members projected musical identities through online names ('Quickfiddler') and avatars as well as through actual text, as seen from this post from the chat forum:

> *Irvine*:   I am a bit of a serial instrumentalist, also play the bouzouki, octave mandola and bodhrán (and a bit of guitar). The bouzouki is great, but there's nothing to compare with playing the tunes on one of the truly traditional instruments.

These identities were defined through participation and ultimately created an OAIM collective identity where, for example, in the above post we saw a member mutually engaging or sharing their learning experiences and ideologies about 'truly traditional instruments' as well as projecting a strong multi-instrumentalist identity. This sharing of knowledge and experiences defined the OAIM practices and fostered participation across cyberspace.

Performance practices also provided significant insights into participation within the CoMPs examined. Here, the groups relied on what Seddon and Biasutti (2009) describe as 'musical communication' where the CoMP learned and negotiated the 'rules' implicitly and explicitly through participatory performance. This was seen very clearly within the jazz ensemble where the improvisatory sections of the per-formances encapsulated a certain 'etiquette' whereby while the improvisations were 'in the moment', they also abided by 'rules' such as: keeping to the tempo, playing for a certain number of bars, and the most experienced players directed the order of individual or small group improvisations (see Chapter 3). The members of both the LJW and CLYC both recounted feelings of 'flow', 'togetherness' and belong-ing' that participatory performance gave to them. For instance, Leona from the jazz ensemble related, 'sometimes you forget you are on stage' while choral member Noreen commented, 'a completely different world and it's just you, the other mem-bers of the choir and Ann'. The members therefore were learning through participa-tion in their 'social world' (Lave & Wenger, 1991) or 'art world' (Becker, 2008).

Membership

'Legitimate peripheral participation' (Lave & Wenger, 1991) is based on an apprenticeship model of learning through membership. 'Newcomers' learn through participation from 'oldtimers' and thus members within CoPs journey from 'peripheral' to 'full' participation. This journey of participation is seen as 'a way of learning – of both absorbing and being absorbed in – the 'culture of prac-tice''' (Lave & Wenger, 1991, p. 95). Role and identity were significant aspects of membership and it was found across all cases that members held multi-member-ships within various musical activities and genres, thus exemplifying the extent of the plurality of their musical identities.

Each CoMP studied had explicit leaders or 'oldtimers' that were cast in those roles for their teaching expertise. For example, Jimmy in the jazz ensemble was the tutor, Ann was the choral director of the CLYC and Kate as co-founder and tutor very much led the OAIM. In each case payment for these skills distinguished them automatically from the rest of the members. While 'expert knowledge' defined these leaders' identity and membership, other social approaches to musical leadership such as nurturing and challenging the groups were viewed as part of the same role.

Ann exemplified a nurturing role as choral director with the CLYC. She was frequently concerned about exam stress for choral members (see Chapter 4) and her nurturing approach was recognised widely among the members: 'she's the reason we come, she's the person that makes us happy' (Karen). Despite the lack of physical contact, a nurturing leadership approach within the OAIM was also observed. One member relayed, 'Love starting one of Kate's videos. When the only instruction you've had is by book, a warm, engaging instructor is a vast improvement – makes me want to practise' (Andy). These leadership skills therefore were multi-faceted, emotionally related to members and musically challenging for the members to sustain their participation.

Wenger writes of 'evolving forms of membership' (Lave & Wenger, 1991, p. 53) within CoPs where the learning cycle within the community moves from peripheral to full participation through apprenticeship learning. Despite the emerging nature of the OAIM as a CoMP, distinctions were observed between 'newcomers' and 'oldtimers' where 'expert knowledge' was sought on the online forums. For instance, Darren posts, 'You mention in more than one lesson to use the 6th or in this case Bm "But Use It Sparingly" . . . So what would one normally play at this point if not the 6th? or is it always ok to use the 6th but only at this point?' Ann, as choral director, rated an apprenticeship form of learning highly within the choir, claiming, 'they're going to learn far more from them [other members] than they are from me' (Ann). Within the CLYC members often spoke of different stages of participation and membership. Chris, for example, recognised, 'I couldn't sing well when I started, now I can'. This sense of moving on a learning trajectory from newcomer to oldtimer was also evident in the LJW where, for instance, Leona commented, 'I have learned so much in my years in the LJW, I find myself giving advice to some of the newer singers'. Longevity and commitment were viewed as an essential part of this evolving membership to all groups where each CoMP built 'shared histories of learning' (Wenger, 1998).

The identities within the group were also formed through membership. For example, the diversity of identities and 'nexus of multi-membership' (Wenger, 1998) individuals carried from other musical communities often defined them within the CoMP. Within the OAIM, multi-membership in other musical communities indicated further members' relationship with music and specifically the Irish traditional music genre. Such multiple musical identities were often articulated through jokes and banter, as was the case in the LJW. For example, in the extract below, we see Jimmy commenting on this multi-membership at a performance:

> Jimmy: I just found out tonight that Enda here once toured with X (*laughter, Enda looks embarrassed*), so we are very privileged to have Enda playing here with us tonight (*audience laughter*).
>
> (LJWVP2)

This joke of course was also imparting values about hierarchies in musical genre as well as letting the audience know that Enda had worked professionally as a musician – albeit in a jovial way. There was a direct swipe at country and western music here as the personality mentioned is a well-known Irish singer in that genre, so this would be seen to please jazz audiences. Jimmy was essentially extending membership of the CoMP to a certain extent here to include audience members, if only for one night. Through dismissing another genre of music, this was meant to bond the audience and members together through a shared love of jazz music. The audience too could then feel a sense of membership in the performance even if it was in the form of 'marginal participation' (Wenger, 1998).

Relationships

Wenger describes an indicator of CoPs as having 'an absence of introductory pre-ambles, as if conversations were merely the continuation of an ongoing process' (1998, p. 125). This was notable within the CLYC and LJW where there were no particular welcoming or parting formalities within rehearsal sessions. There was also little to no lead-in time in discussing what would be played/sung or how. Such interactions, customary exchanges and practices indicated the formation of a CoMP where evidence of 'sustained mutual relationships', 'shared ways of engaging' and 'absence of introductory preambles' (Wenger, 1998) was present.

Relationships emerged as crucial for CoMP development and sustainability within the three cases. In the case of the OAIM, as an emerging community this was particularly important. The formation of such relationships was revealed through interactions, in very obvious ways through the online chat forums and Facebook page. Here, knowledge-sharing, 'in-jokes' and making personal con-nections were evident. Particular to the online case was a shared affinity with Ireland and its traditions within the genre which helped create a particular col-lective identity between members. This was demonstrated within the chat forums and Facebook page through posts where knowledge was shared about musical performers and festivals, and some posts were written in the Irish language.

As well as between participants, there were teacher/learner relationships to be discerned through musical and social interactions within the CoMP. For instance, within the jazz ensemble, Jimmy as tutor had a much more distinct teacher/learner relationship with the singers than the instrumentalists. The pedagogical style shifted with the singers who were provided with (and sought) greater leader-ship, instruction and praise than the instrumentalists. This could be attributed to a number of factors including a distinction between singers and instrumentalists, and the fact that the singers were the only females in the group, less experienced than the instrumentalists and only joined the group for the latter half of rehearsal.

Within the CLYC, the teacher/learner relationship between the choral director and members was clearly defined. Ann held 'expert knowledge' in the group evi-denced through the structure of rehearsals, choice of repertoire, starting and stop-ping singing, conducting, instructing and gesturing. The OAIM was also clear in the marked difference within the community between teacher and learner, where video tutorials were provided by the tutors and paid for by members. This knowledge was respected and valued where, for example, Matt related, 'I feel connected to a person who clearly knows what she is doing. The fact that she is so qualified to teach is really important to me'.

Jokes and laughter were highly significant to the relationships observed and functioned across the three cases as a means of fun, to create a sense of belonging, define identities and relationships or very often as actual tools for learning. Within the LJW jazz lore often entailed humorous anecdotes about jazz 'masters' or genre-specific conventions (see Chapter 3). However, the diversity within the group was also often referred to in a joke or banter-like manner as seen in the interaction below:

Jimmy: How do you think it went when we did it last week?
Leona: It was fine, I didn't like myself very much but that is maybe –
Jimmy: It's an Italian guilt thing is it? (laughs)
Leona: What not liking oneself? (laughter)
Jimmy: You are too close to the Vatican you see (laughter)
Leona: We'll never get rid of it . . .

(LJWV2)

This exchange was indicative of the casual, jovial social interactions within the ensemble and indicated sustained, built-up, close-knit relationships within this CoMP.

Socio-musical interactions were also significant to the theme of relationships. Ann, as choral director of a youth choir, was acutely aware of the importance of the social dimension to the members. This building of relationships to form a sense of 'belonging', she related, was vital as 'you want them to feel that they are coming to some place where they can be themselves, where they are comfortable' (Ann). The jazz ensemble was more heavily focused on musical interactions than social interactions (though still interlinked) which was probably due to the age profile of the group as more mature than the choir. These interactions were characterised by certain routines, behaviours, cues and gestures. Taking the performance interactions only, these were observed through 'conventions' (Becker, 2008) such as: the positioning of the ensemble, the format of the tunes and solo improvisation sections, the banter and 'insider' jokes, and certain musical cues such as touching the head to return to the main tune.

Reflections

All three CoMPs developed in particular ways and approaches that were unique to each community's identity and domain. 'Shared knowledge' was created and built through mutual engagement where the learning was 'situated', 'authentic' and grounded in 'real world' practices (Koopman, 2007; Lave & Wenger, 1991; Robson, 2002). The characteristics of identity-building, collective knowledge and belonging were significant across the themes discussed and can be summarised thus:

- Identity: was revealed to be a key characteristic for a CoMP to occur and sustain itself where members formed identities through their membership.
- Collective knowledge: was evidenced to be built up collaboratively through an apprenticeship model of learning within the three CoMPs.
- Belonging: was acquired through a social apprenticeship process of learning where both individual as well as collective identities were formed.

Joint enterprise

Within the CoP model Wenger describes joint enterprise as a *process* among a community of people where there is: a 'negotiated enterprise', 'an indigenous enterprise' and a 'regime of mutual accountability' (1998, pp. 77–82). This section will examine this process through an investigation of all three of these characteristics.

Negotiated enterprise

The three CoMPs examined went through an ongoing 'process of negotiation' (Wenger, 1998, p. 77) through shared practices to create a common 'joint enterprise'. This was revealed most starkly within the jazz and choral communities where throughout rehearsal sessions and performances members negotiated responses to situations to make music and perform collectively. Within the LJW such practices as starting late for rehearsal sessions exemplified this negotiation. The stated start time was 7pm but in reality the members themselves negotiated this time by communally accepting that not everyone would arrive then. There were no consequences for poor punctuality and no one ever complained.

Musical signifiers within the CLYC such as gestures from the choral director to stay together, add interpretative nuances or re-establish pitch were negotiated 'in the moment' (see Chapter 4). The negotiation of such gestures was also apparent in the LJW where, for example, during a performance Jimmy non-verbally assigned solo sequences to the ensemble, Jack often set the tempo using his beaters, solos were improvised and a return to the main tune was guided by either Jack or Jimmy through non-verbal gestures such as nods, touching their heads or playing out the main tune very loudly for the others to join in after a few notes were played (see Chapter 3). This all occurred through musical communication between the members of the CoMP within the performance itself, negotiated as required 'in the moment' to reach the desired musical output or 'joint enterprise'.

Collective decision-making also required a process of negotiation within all three CoMPs. This was seen, for example, in the questions and requests put to the tutors in the chat forums within the OAIM. These interactions resulted in the development of learner supports such as notation and mp3 files. For instance, Lotti posted on the chat forum, 'Regarding sheet music, although I try to get the tunes by ear, which is relatively easy taking into account that you teach them in very short phrases and slowly . . . I prefer to have the sheet paper at hand!' Co-founder Kate also described the input of one member, an e-learning specialist, who heavily influenced the learning system of the OAIM through his feedback.

These types of requests and feedback from the members of the community formed part of the negotiated enterprise of developing the teaching and learning directions within the OAIM. As an emerging CoMP, it was vitally important that such input was recognised and valued to create a sense of 'joint enterprise'; Wenger asserts, 'they must find a way to do that together' (1998, p. 79).

Although Ann as choral director within the CLYC was the obvious leader, collective decision-making was present to a degree within the choir too. Shared practices such as self-evaluation (for example, making judgements on the sound quality, pitch or pace of a song) and problem-solving (such as deciding where to breathe or when to fade out) during rehearsals exemplified such negotiated collaborative input. The below extract taken from the LJW video data also demonstrated collective decisions that were often negotiated within the jazz ensemble CoMP:

Jimmy:	(referring to an upcoming performance) Anybody want to do it in a specific order? We've got five tunes isn't it?
Eric:	Yeah I think the one 'Interplay' should go at the end because it's the one everybody does
Jimmy:	Yeah sure
Eric:	Everyone's involved
Jimmy:	That's the last one
Jack:	Start with the 'Prism', it's a nice one to start with
Jimmy:	and what's the other two? We've got three other songs then
Jack:	There's one we have, Jackle
Eric:	Jackle
Jimmy:	'Taste of Honey' maybe in the middle . . .

(LJWV10)

From the extract, we see a clear, shared negotiated decision-making process occurring here. Jimmy, although the tutor, encouraged suggestions and mutual leadership. Jack and Eric as fellow 'oldtimers' joined in this process. The other members, however, appeared content to allow the more established members work through this process, signifying their 'legitimate peripheral participation' (Wenger, 1998).

The 'joint enterprise' of the jazz ensemble emerged as ranging from learning/advancing their playing of jazz music, playing within a collective, building confidence to play in new ways, enjoying themselves and performing in live situations. These shared goals went through an ongoing 'process of negotiation' (Wenger, 1998, p. 77) throughout the rehearsal sessions and performances as with the other two CoMPs. For instance, Jimmy constantly challenged the group to play more creatively, experiment and 'tune in' to each other while playing. Leona noted a re-adjusting or negotiation of expectations from when she initially joined the group, 'All I had expected was just regular practice and perhaps learning some new songs. Over the years it has become much more challenging, as the band has progressed as well'.

The rehearsal sessions functioned as a preparation for the 'joint enterprise' of performance within both the jazz ensemble and youth choir. The performances served to demonstrate musical progression within both communities but were also noted to be a vital part of members' enjoyment within their respective CoMP. The choir noted the significant impact that performance had on their enjoyment as individuals and as a collective. For example, one member commented, 'It makes me feel amazing, I feel such a rush when I am with them' (Amy) while Joey wrote, 'It feels great! There's a feeling of togetherness and dependency'. This resonated with the LJW performances too where, for instance, Jack commented on the collective negotiation of 'tuning in' required to reach the desired 'joint enterprise' of musical output, 'Your ears, just you have to be logically number one, aware of what's happening around you and then the other thing you've got to think about is who is playing what at what time'.

Indigenous enterprise

Taking the constructionist viewpoints underpinning this study (see Chapter 1), the notion of a CoP having an indigenous enterprise is not surprising where learning is seen as 'situated' (Elliott, 1995; Koopman, 2007; Scardamalia & Bereiter, 1991). In this way learning occurred through interaction and local responses where 'participation is always based on situated negotiation and renegotiation of meaning in the world' (Lave & Wenger, 1991, p. 51).

Context is important within the indigenous enterprise. This concept was most interesting to consider within the online case study, the OAIM. There was a strong sense within this CoMP of approaching, negotiating and developing Irish traditional music tuition in new ways through online learning. The accessibility the OAIM afforded to 'local' high-quality Irish traditional music tuition was seen as hugely beneficial where one tutor remarked:

> I think getting lessons directly from someone who is living in Clare is a lot closer to a notional 'source' than a lot of people get by internet or live means outside of Ireland . . . if you're living somewhere without access to quality traditional musicians, this is quite close to a direct line to very high quality teachers.

> (Ben)

The 'indigenous enterprise' that this extract related marked out the distinctively 'Irish identity' of the OAIM as explored in Chapter 5. Existing in cyberspace, one is tempted to view the CoMP as devoid of a physical or geographical context, yet the OAIM very much promoted a Clare-based, west of Ireland identity that revealed itself from such aspects as the choice of tutors to the visual images presented on the website and Facebook page depicting rural Irish landscapes. The 'cybersession' also highlighted the importance of 'indigenous enterprise' to the CoP. Here, live traditional music performance in a local context was accessed over cyberspace through live streaming. Kate, the co-founder, commented:

it was really an embodiment of the traditional session and it was fairly much a session, it wasn't rehearsed . . . it was massively important because it really on a local level it stated who we are, what we're doing as well as on an international level.

As an online community, this identity was a transnational one, negotiated in and through the CoMP practices.

The LJW existed within Limerick city, the mid-west of Ireland, which was relevant to the sociocultural, geographical and political landscape of the jazz ensemble. The workshop in their name itself projected such an identity. The fact the group was outside of Dublin was often referred to as a disadvantage for jazz playing and performance, and the members were aware of this. Jimmy commented, 'the opportunities for people living in Dublin are massive compared to down here'. Furthermore, the political and economic landscape the ensemble rested within was evident through a sense of resignation about depleting supports for the arts where Jimmy mentioned the financial state of the country as a major barrier to future supports, stating that Ireland was 'in a post-war economy'. Furthermore, the racial and cultural diversity of the group reflected a European dimension with four nationalities represented in the membership. Eric jokingly commented, 'we are like the United Nations'. All of this built a localised collective identity for the jazz ensemble which was negotiated in response to their situation and as such 'belongs to them' (Wenger, 1998, p. 77).

The significance of context for the study of the youth choir was also very strong, with its identity also punctuated in its name – the County Limerick Youth Choir. The choir as an initiative of Limerick County Council (now Limerick City and County Council) had very obvious connections with its local context. This was highlighted during their performances where they represented the local government arts office. In particular, the choir's performance for the Éigse festival saw a culmination of an 'indigenous enterprise' between the choir and arts office to devise the programme to perform at the festival. The collaborative relationship between the arts officer, choral director and choir members was revealed as hugely important to this process. The local government identity was recognised as important to its members, with one member stating, 'it brings a sense of pride to it, we kind of represent Limerick youth' (Joey).

Mutual accountability

Across all three cases, 'mutual accountability' was fostered and developed. This was often facilitated by the 'oldtimers' or experts. Jimmy, for instance, invited the members to begin playing in each rehearsal session of the LJW. However, Jimmy also often cast himself as a learner in the group, where for instance he admitted in rehearsal, 'So maybe do it slow enough 'cause I don't know the bass line' (LJWV3). This form of learning, referenced by Wenger as 'horizontalization' (Wenger, 2006), enabled peer-to-peer learning among the CoMP members.

Despite the leaders in each CoMP guiding the learning and performances, there was an immense sense of group responsibility or 'mutual accountability' (Wenger, 1998). Within the CLYC, members noted this sense of group responsibility where 'everyone must do their job' (Nancy) and 'we all work together to make something great' (Conor). This collective sense of group responsibility was also observed in the OAIM despite existing in cyberspace where connections were made in relation to collaborative musical learning. Alice commented, 'The enthusiasm of others encourages me to keep at it and learn and delve more deeply into playing the music'. 'Mutual accountability' was also very prominent in the LJW where members recorded not enjoying their membership within the ensemble if they were absent or not 'up to standard'. Leona, for example, recorded a feeling of guilt and being 'disappointed and annoyed' at not being able to fulfil her membership role in the LJW fully due to work constraints. Eric questioned his musical skills to rise to the challenging playing and hoped not to 'let down the other group members'.

A shared learning approach through horizontal structures was also evident in the OAIM where, for example, Kate requested collaborative input through the online forums into the making of the video tutorials (see Chapter 5). As well as this, it was noted that the online forums encouraged the sharing of musical and social experiences, feedback, progression updates and knowledge. Kate, as 'oldtimer', consistently encouraged 'newcomers' to join in the development of a 'joint enterprise' within the online forums, where, for example, she posts, 'If any of you have requests for tunes you would like me to teach in my next course – let me know'. This 'negotiation of mutual relevance' (Wenger, 2006, p. 29) recognised different forms of knowledge between members where knowledge was shared, negotiated and used to build a shared practice within the CoMP.

Reflections

The direction, focus and structure of the three CoMPs as they evolved were very much shaped by the members of the communities. The members ultimately went through an ongoing 'process of negotiation' of 'joint enterprise' (Wenger, 1998, p. 77) within their practices throughout the data fieldwork period. Key aspects of 'negotiated enterprise', 'indigenous enterprise' and 'mutual accountability' were presented under the dimension of joint enterprise within the CoP model. The characteristics of identity and 'horizontalization' were significant across the three communities and can be summarised as:

- Identity: negotiating an identity as a member of a CoMP as well as projecting a collective local identity was emphasised as key to the joint enterprise of these communities.
- Collective knowledge: 'horizontalization' was found to be crucial where shared learning, collaborative input and collective decision-making were essential to the sustainability of the three CoMPs.
- Belonging: was engendered within the CoMP through particular contextualised responses to each local situation. Mutual accountability in particular fostered this.

Shared repertoire

Taking the view that 'the repertoire of a community is a resource for the negotia-tion of meaning' (Wenger, 1998, p. 84), the interactions and discourses of such a community are important to the building of a CoMP. Aspects of shared repertoire transpired through distinct discourses within each case which were employed as both musical learning tools as well as socialisation mechanisms within the com-munities. These are classified here as the use of jokes and laughter, lore, as well as a range of learning tools to illuminate the importance of a shared repertoire to a community's coherence. This repertoire was developed and negotiated through shared ways of doing things or practices among the jazz ensemble, youth choir and online community.

Jokes and laughter

Jokes and laughter made up a significant part of the three CoMP shared ways of doing things (102 references were coded to 'jokes/laughter' across 24 sources within the NVivo analysis). This was repeatedly evidenced as being an essential part of membership within the three communities and also acted as a motivation to stay involved. Jokes and laughter often functioned as learning tools in them-selves, to promote a casual atmosphere, to reinforce traditions and values as well as to promote a feeling of belonging. Table 6.2 outlines examples across all three communities to exemplify these functions.

As seen from the table, jokes and laughter served varying functions across the cases. As learning tools, for instance, Jimmy used jokes referencing jazz 'master' Miles Davis to impart values about improvisation to the LJW. Ann attempted to get across the notion of learning through scaffolding, reassuring the CLYC through banter that the piece of music would sound better as they became more familiar with it. Within the OAIM chat forum, Irvine joked about the lack of phys-ical contact within the e-learning tools provided through video tutorials, again in a very jovial style. Jokes about e-learning became a regular feature of interactions on the online chat forums.

This attention to jokes and laughter created a distinctive casual atmosphere within each CoMP. Such 'in-jokes', according to Wenger, are a regular feature of cultivating 'communities of practice' as one indicator of building a 'shared repertoire' between participants (Wenger, 1998). Ewing (2008, p. 581) also states, 'using jokes and memes is a way for new members to show they understand the culture'. This casual atmosphere, illustrated through the examples in Table 6.2, where we see the use of bad language, fun made of song titles and joking self-deprecation, was created through social interactions – essentially through laugh-ter, jokes, friendships and chat demonstrated throughout the data fieldwork across the three cases.

Often the jokes and laughter centred on genre-specific or at least music-specific topics and so values and traditions were reinforced through their use. For example, Enda and Jimmy's exchange in Table 6.2 illustrated the multi-membership Enda

Table 6.2 Cross-comparison of the functions of 'jokes and laughter' within CoMPs

Category	Samples from cross-case comparison		
	LJW*	CLYC**	OAIM***
Learning tools	Jimmy: someone said to him [Miles Davis] once, 'why don't you play that stuff anymore? He said, 'I thought we got it right the first time.' (LJWV9)	Marianne: It's awful Ann: It's not awful (plays notes). You're allowed your opinion but you'll be fine once you know it Marianne: You're wrong Ann: And I'm allowed to disagree. (CLYCV3)	Irvine: I am puzzled how you can see what I am doing because you keep saying 'good'! (OAIM chat forum)
Casual atmosphere	Jimmy: Derek Bailey claimed a giant wrestler screaming in your face because you fucked around with the entrance from the theme to the Gladiator is the best argument against improvisation I've ever heard. (LJWV1)	Ann: We will have to all be together that we can do 'O Holy Night' and maybe 'the Joy to Curls' (CLYCV1)	Doc E Doc: I'll poke it into my player and set repeat to, say, a few thousand cycles. That should scrape some grooves into my memory (OAIM chat forum)
Reinforce tradition/value	Enda: it's hard to get a handle on it without a person keeping a beat Jimmy: You're too used to bodhrán players. (LJWV7)	Ann: If you stop, stop . . . don't just suddenly get loud again! (CLYCV7)	Kate: I am not sure what the temperature is like in Minnesota, but it can be chilly (especially indoors) in Ireland and I won't practise without a cuppa! (OAIM chat forum)
Promote belonging	Jimmy: if you were doing it for the money you might have to worry about what people think . . . if somebody told you there was money in this they lied. (LJWV1)	Kristen: Will it be just us [in reference to Christmas performance]? Ann: Well no – Santa Claus will be there too (CLYCV2)	Tommy60: 'I think Flute Progressives is grammatically correct, Kate, but it does sound a little like a new political party, lol, and one I would certainly join and campaign for ☺ (OAIM chat forum)

*LJW: Limerick Jazz Workshop
**CLYC: County Limerick Youth Choir
***OAIM: Online Academy of Irish Music

held as a musician that bridged both Irish traditional and jazz 'musical worlds' (Finnegan, 2007). Jimmy poked fun at this multi-membership in a friendly manner, but also in doing so instilled an essential difference of tradition between the two genres, where jazz does not rely on a steady beat. The CLYC extracts from the table illustrated the manner in which the choir regularly dealt with mistakes – with jovial discourse. Through jokes and laughter, Ann promoted the value of responding to markings on the score in classical music. Homely colloquial terms such as 'cuppa' within the OAIM chat forum projected a distinct sense of the 'local', thereby in this context reinforcing the 'Irishness' (O'Flynn, 2009) associated with the genre of Irish traditional music.

A sense of belonging was also developed among the communities through the use of jokes and laughter. Ann's joke about Santa Claus also being present at the Christmas concert (evidenced in Table 6.2) reflected the close-knit nature of the CLYC. Shared jokes and laughter also created a sense of belonging among the LJW. Jimmy's jibe in Table 6.2 at no money to be gained through jazz music also saw a loyalty and belonging among members to the jazz genre, despite no promise of financial gain. The OAIM extract in Table 6.2 illustrated the use of 'in-jokes' on the chat forum which often centred on the Irish traditional genre itself. Thus, references to genre-specific terminology created among the CoMPs functioned not just as amusing anecdotes but also helped to project a collective identity or belonging to the genre, as well as the distinctive musical communities.

Lore

The use of lore as a resource within the CoMPs (defined here as anecdotes, stories and jokes) was especially prevalent among the jazz ensemble. The jazz domain or music-making of the LJW carried genre-specific conventions, norms, language use, jargon, stories, jokes, values and traditions. Jimmy as tutor stood as the 'expert' in the domain of jazz and so facilitated induction into this 'jazz world' through discourse within musical and social processes. This approach to teaching and learning was most evident in Jimmy's consistent use of jazz lore.

Jazz lore was employed by tutor Jimmy to articulate his vision for the ensemble to become more creative in their playing through musical challenges and so acted as an important learning tool within the ensemble. This jazz lore usually employed references to jazz 'legends' or 'masters' to inspire and promote experimentation (see Chapter 3). The extract below illustrated further the use of jazz lore as a learning tool and means of enculturation to the 'jazz world'. Revisiting part of this extract, Jimmy claimed:

> I remember Kenny Werner said once, "the tradition of jazz is innovation". That's the actual tradition of it and it's not reproducing stuff that you know over and over again. All the great jazz players – every one of them got slated probably at the time for certain things they were doing because they were doing something different . . . So you know you'll be dead long enough really.
>
> (LJWV1)

Such stories and anecdotes generally appeared to make Jimmy's vision for the ensemble more meaningful for the members where, as seen above, the message behind the story is that the members should not be afraid to experiment more in their playing. The members responded quite well to such lore which could be heard in their subsequent playing. The members essentially 'negotiated' such resources to make meaning collectively and make such lore relevant to their situation and playing.

Jimmy, as an 'oldtimer', employed this lore as a significant mechanism to impart and mediate learning about such musical elements of style, technique and structure but also just as significantly about the principles and values of jazz music. The below extract of Jimmy talking to singer Beatrice shows one further example of this:

> *Jimmy*: (to Beatrice) the lyrics in front of you are a blockage in terms of trying to communicate something to people and it's also the fact you're looking at lyrics and not looking around you at other people . . . I remember playing with a singer once and my uncle was on drums and she had a tendency not to make any contact with anybody, just stay straight out front but she used to get lost on the solos, she wouldn't know where to come back in . . . eventually my uncle at a gig one night, he got a flag made up with the word 'NOW' written on it (everyone laughs) and about two bars before she was due back in he'd just shout her name and start waving the flag – and it still didn't work (everyone laughs).
>
> (LJWV9)

Jimmy here through jazz lore emphasised the need in jazz music for group contact during playing. It was evident that he really felt it was important for Beatrice to learn such elements of the 'jazz trade' but equally he was involving everyone in the group through his 'storytelling'. In this manner, Jimmy was engaging in a discourse that involves what Lave and Wenger describe as 'talking about' and 'talking within' a practice (1991, p. 109) where, for example, information is 'talked about', 'within' a story.

Although the use of lore as a form of shared repertoire was most prominent within the jazz ensemble, there were some instances of its use in the OAIM too. Stories and anecdotes regarding well-known recordings, teachers and performers in the Irish traditional genre served a similar function as the 'jazz masters' within the LJW. The following conversation from a chat forum demonstrates another such use of lore:

> *Quickfiddler*: I have been playing fiddle and flute for about 25 years and through most of that I have struggled to find good instructors (very hard to find here in Vancouver) . . . I really love the fact that you teach the traditional philosophy that you can't learn the air unless you know what they're singing about. Can't separate the music from the language. More power to ya. ☺

Monica:	I am really glad that you agree with my idea of making sure to have the words and background to the airs. I have had so many debates with people over this topic. I have a serious passion for airs and it is something that I will not compromise on . . .
Quickfiddler:	That's why my old teacher (Tomas Stand Evan) wouldn't let me near a tune without knowing its history and if there was an air related to it I had to make sure that I had done my research. Not only was Tomas my fiddle/flute teacher he was also the Gaelic instructor.

As well as sharing musical background and knowledge, there was an attempt here through lore to project individual identities and traditional ideologies. In particular, Monica projected strongly held beliefs in relation to background information on Irish airs. We also gain insight into existing tensions and debates among Irish traditional musicians on such issues. For instance, 'it is something that I will not compromise on' suggested Monica's perceived need to advocate for words and contextual information to accompany airs. Such an ideology resonated with Quickfiddler and the way he was taught, again referencing a teacher to make a connection to the tutor.

Learning tools

Learning tools were shaped and developed collectively through the CoMPs as resources for making music. Within the CLYC learning tools of sight-singing, guided instruction from the choral director and split vocal section work illustrated the choir's scaffolded approach to shared learning. For example, gestures from the choral director such as clicking, conducting time, indicating entries and cut-offs, as well as playing notes on the keyboard to re-establish pitch were employed often. These learning tools were employed with familiarity and fluidity within the youth choir, indicating a shared history of collective knowledge among the members.

The OAIM promoted the use of online technologies for the development of learning tools within the community. The e-learning system saw: video tutorials employing an Irish traditional music pedagogy (through aural and oral transmission), sheet music, mp3 listening files and notation as support materials, as well as the discussion forums for members. Technique, skills and style were developed or scaffolded through the repertoire taught. The learning through oral transmission, though online, was very dominant in keeping with the traditional culture of the genre.

Recordings of jazz music emerged as important learning tools for the LJW and this had been in-built in their shared practice. Listening to jazz recordings was regarded as just as important a learning tool as notation. These 'artifacts' within the group linked directly to the reverence often given to the jazz 'legends' in jazz lore explored earlier. Jimmy stressed the need for the members to listen to such recordings often and commented, 'the ear is a muscle as well, it has to be exercised'. Members too noted their importance, where they described their practising habits outside of rehearsal sessions as heavily reliant on recordings. This use of recordings to influence their playing and singing and gain further jazz knowledge therefore developed as a shared repertoire between the members of the jazz ensemble both individually and collectively. This resonated with a finding by Karlsen who related that 'intellectual-musical tools' were both style-specific as well as contextually and communally dependent (2010, p. 40).

The practising habits of the youth choir members also noted significant links with recordings as learning tools where members listened to pieces on iPods and YouTube. This use of new technology was of course also very prominent within the online CoMP. E-learning tools such as YouTube and software to slow down a tune were specifically employed during members' practising routines. These tools complemented the actual e-learning tools provided on the OAIM website of video tutorials and mp3 files. Often links to free Internet recordings and resources were also shared between members on the chat forums and Facebook page.

Reflections

Through investigating shared repertoire which can be described as the 'frame-works, ideas, tools, information, styles, languages, stories and documents that community members share' (Wenger, et al., 2002, p. 29), further insights into the identities and practices of the three CoMPs were explored. The shared repertoire was distinct and 'belonged' to each CoMP which was illuminated in how they employed jokes, laughter, lore and learning tools discussed in this section. The characteristics of identity, belonging and collective knowledge were significant across the three characteristics and can be summarised thus:

- Identity: emerged as important to the development of shared repertoire where members used and mediated the discourses within their communities to form both individual and collective identities.
- Collective knowledge: was then built up through such a process of shared input where members negotiated meaning through practice.
- Belonging: was also very strong in the shared repertoire between each CoMP as it involved a collective sharing and participation of resources.

Summary

This chapter sought to bring together a cross-case comparison using the CoP framework as an analytical and interpretive lens to the study. Holmes and Meyerhoff claim (1999, p. 181), 'the CoP concept offers a potentially productive means of linking micro-level and macro-level analyses'. Key characteristics of CoMPs across the three cases are illustrated in Figure 6.1 below (adapted from Wenger, 1998, p. 5):

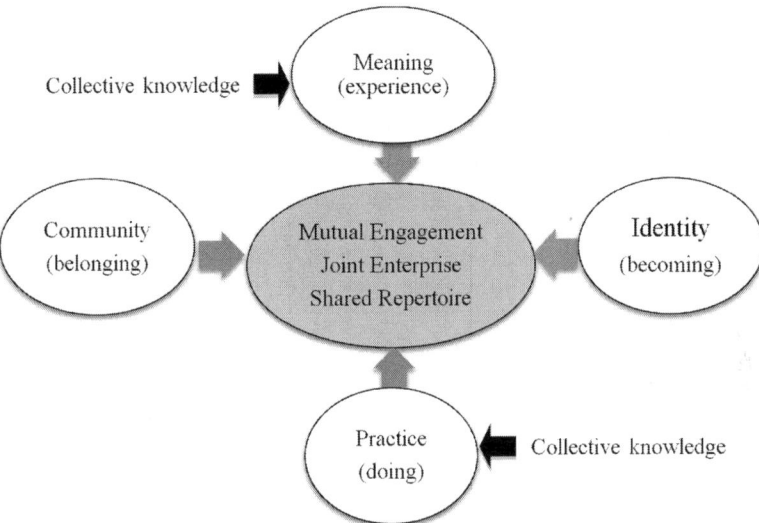

Figure 6.1 Summary of cross-case comparison within CoP framework

Key findings related to identity, collective knowledge and belonging were very significant across all three dimensions of mutual engagement, joint enterprise and shared repertoire within the CoMP examined. Each case remained distinctive and 'situated' within their specific domains and practices to capitalise on local resources. A sense of belonging, collaborative learning and identity-building were all key to each community's development and sustainability. These characteristics were deemed to be mutually dependent in that through a social apprenticeship process of learning that is collaborative or shared, members form identities and acquire a sense of belonging. This highlighted the importance of a sociocultural learning system within musical communities.

7 Fostering communities of musical practice

> The Caterpillar and Alice looked at each other for some time in silence: at last the Caterpillar took the hookah out of its mouth, and addressed her in a languid, sleepy voice.
>
> 'Who are *YOU*?' said the Caterpillar.
>
> This was not an encouraging opening for a conversation. Alice replied, rather shyly, 'I – I hardly know, sir, just at present – at least I know who I *WAS* when I got up this morning, but I think I must have been changed several times since then.'
>
> 'What do you mean by that?' said the Caterpillar sternly. 'Explain yourself!'
>
> 'I can't explain *MYSELF*, I'm afraid, sir,' said Alice, 'because I'm not myself, you see.'
>
> (Carroll, 2009)

Alice is in a new world, a 'wonderland', confronted by all manner of creatures, characters and episodes. Due to her encounters she is experiencing an identity crisis, struggling to interpret and make meaning from her experiences. She is lost in a dream and cannot go back. In this context she is challenged to question her relationship and way of being in the world. With each encounter, she has to learn and negotiate the rules to 'play the game', thus adapting to social situations. As she masters each challenge on this journey, she grows wiser and assimilates into her new community. One could claim in this sense, she is transformed.

This book has offered a means of understanding the nature of communities of musical practice (CoMPs) and their potential for transformation in community and educational contexts. Through distinctive illustrations presented, members of these communities were shown to engage in a process of collective music-making that was at once both musical and social. Akin to Alice, they encounter new situations and characters, they learn, negotiate and interpret 'the rules', and in doing so make meaning from their experiences to inform (and potentially transform) their individual and collective identities. The power of these communities as a rich music education resource and sustainable model for musical participation is particularly highlighted throughout the book. Thus, recommendations for fostering CoMPs are put forward in this final chapter with specific reference to both policy and practice.

Transformation through communities of musical practice

The three illustrations presented in this book have demonstrated how CoMPs formed in and through musical, community and distinctive practices. These practices did not manifest in a vacuum, however, but were evidenced as medi-ated by context. The context was underpinned by economic, social and cultural remits, while the practices were underpinned by distinctive characteristics of identity, collective knowledge and belonging within a community of practice (CoP) framework. The evidence suggests that CoMPs are nested within practices and contexts where one cannot be separated from the other. As John-Steiner reminds us (2000, p. 202):

> The sustainability of a collaboration depends on the supporting structures in which it is embedded . . . . The field consists of the institutions and individu-als that select and support innovations within a domain . . . . These in turn are affected by the socio-political atmosphere.

Each musical community developed in response to local circumstances and as such this was distinctive to each case. For instance, the youth choir examined was initiated and sustained through local government policy, the jazz ensemble arose from a need to access teaching and performance opportunities in the mid-west of Ireland, while the Online Academy of Irish Music sought to go beyond the local (while staying rooted to a local identity) in expanding the teaching of traditional music to an online space.

Key characteristics of the CoMP practices emerged as identity, collective knowledge and belonging. The presence of these characteristics was found to be crucial to the development of practices within the cases studied and can be sum-marised as follows:

Identity: Collective as well as individual identities were formed and projected through interactions within the CoMPs. These were manifested through musical, community and distinctive practices. Thus, the members within their respective communities held both identities congruently.

Collective knowledge: Members within the CoMPs built up knowledge through shared, collaborative experiences. Musical and community practices developed in an interrelated manner largely through a shared learning approach. As such, one type of practice could not be valued over the other where the experiences were socio-musical.

Belonging: A sense of belonging among the members permeated throughout the CoMPs investigated. This was evidenced through socio-musical interactions where members' participation formed and sustained practices. Hence, belonging was central to membership within a CoMP.

The findings revealed these three characteristics as mutually dependent to sustain each community's practices and fed into the three dimensions of CoPs: mutual engagement, joint enterprise and shared repertoire (outlined in Chapter 6). Figure 7.1 illustrates the situated and interrelated nature of CoMPs.

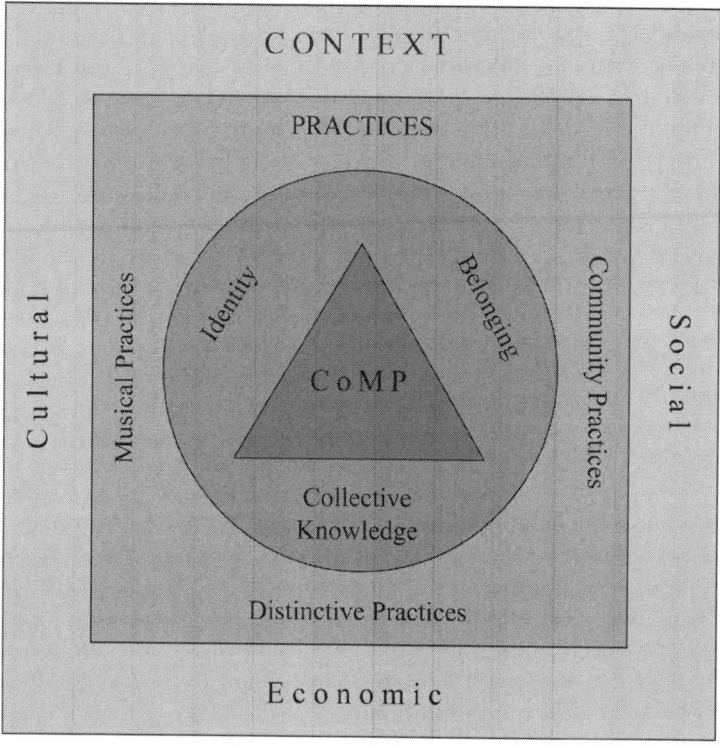

Figure 7.1 Situating communities of musical practice

In analysing three communities in-depth in one geographical area, the analysis was rooted in micro practices but located within the broader macro framework of local, national and international contexts. Taking the sociocultural lens applied to this research, Becker reminds us, 'For someone who thinks sociologically . . . it can mean seeing everything as an instance of collective activity, as the result of many people and institutions acting together' (1998, p. 216). Figure 7.1 demonstrates this 'collective activity' that surrounds CoMPs where distinctive characteristics are embedded within practices, which are embedded within contexts. All levels interact to varying degrees to inform (or inhibit) the development of CoMPs. These characteristics were deemed to be mutually dependent in that through a social apprenticeship process of learning that is collaborative or shared, members form identities and acquire a sense of belonging. The importance of a sociocultural learning system within musical communities is thus highlighted. A mapping of the main findings informing the conclusions of Figure 7.1 is located in Appendix D.

Maxine Greene (1982, 1995, 2001) continually reminds us of the enormous possibilities deep engagement with an art form can hold for transformation. Music as participatory social action extends such engagement into collaborative forms, where the impact can affect both individual and community. Greene argues that such a community 'ought to be a space infused by the kind of imaginative awareness that enables those involved to imagine alternative possibilities for their own becoming and their group's becoming' (1995, p. 39). CoMPs offer a means of such deep engagement and 'becoming' with music, where the music made becomes inseparable from the people who make it. This book highlights that CoMPs cannot be decreed but rather only CoMPs themselves can develop their own distinct 'situated' practices. However, music educationalists, community music facilitators, teachers, administrators and policy-makers can certainly facilitate, foster and enable CoMPs within their many communities. In this way, we all hold the potential to create spaces for transformation to occur.

Recommendations for policy and practice

The findings from the CoMPs explored in this book highlight the importance of group music-making opportunities in people's lives. If, as Countryman claims, 'music educators cannot construct or mandate communities of practice – rather foster' (2009, p. 106), this research has uncovered significant insights and implications into how sustainable CoMPs may be fostered from policy and practice perspectives. Policy recommendations are put forward here for local, national and international policy-makers with a view to influencing future directions for not only developing potential CoMPs but also sustaining such communities.

Recommendations for policy

1   Increase local control for CoMPs in policy to achieve a closer policy-practice partnership that is mutually informative.
2   Allow time to build relationships between policy and practice to ensure open dialogue between both.
3   Adopt a mediation role where CoMPs are not bound by policy but rather enabled by it.
4   Capitalise on local resources and expertise to shape and inform CoMPs.
5   Be flexible enough to tailor the support required by differing CoMPs – such decisions should be decided at a local level.
6   Funding and support mechanisms need to take a long-term view of CoMP development to provide stability and sustainability.
7   Provide multiple and varied 'spaces' for CoMPs to ensure broadened inclusion opportunities for musical engagement.
8   Research and evaluation needs to play a far more integral role in CoMPs to inform future developments and decisions.

Recommendations for practice are also presented to inform potential, emerging and existing CoMPs. These are put forward for both community and educational contexts that too often are seen as oppositional. These recommendations seek to inform all manner of music education and community music contexts whether formal, nonformal or informal, or as is often the case, where many of these approaches co-exist. The implications of the research findings for music practice emphasise the need to foster a sense of belonging, inform identities and promote collective knowledge between members within CoMPs and so these characteristics permeate throughout the recommendations.

Recommendations for practice

1   Provide inclusive group music-making opportunities where membership and participation are promoted.
2   Promote and value socio-musical relationships and interactions where collective and individual identities are nurtured. Time is particularly required for this development.
3   Employ formal, nonformal and informal approaches to the teaching and learning of music. Musically challenging the members is important for sustained participation and progression.
4   Appreciate differing levels of participation and collaboration.
5   Link educational institutions with community initiatives to increase opportunities for overlapping and complementary CoMPs.
6   Emphasise learning as an endeavour of knowledge-building, sharing, and negotiation where meaning-making is both collaborative and 'situated'.
7   Promote reflective practice at group and individual levels.
8   Foster positive values and attitudes towards musical engagement as well as skills acquisition to foster life-long CoMP participation.

The recommendations present challenges for policy and practice in their implications for how we view musical teaching and learning. For policy, the imperative to balance bottom-up (informed by local practices) and top-down (informed by international, national and local policies) approaches within a policy-practice interface is emphasised. Within communities, music-making needs to seek a balance between social and musical interactions where challenge and learning are valued as core components of participation.

Formal educational institutions and conservatoires may find the recommendations particularly challenging when working under curriculum and assessment constraints. However, the insights gleaned from the study establish the importance of the characteristics of identity, collective knowledge and a sense of belonging within CoMPs as rooted within a sociocultural theory of learning. Wenger (1998, p. 85) explains, 'Communities of practice . . . are a force to be reckoned with . . . such communities hold the key to real transformation – the kind that has real effects on people's lives'.

Pedagogical implications then point to the need for reconsidering teaching approaches and perspectives to re-imagine classrooms as spaces for CoMPs to occur. Members within the communities examined consistently demonstrated a love and deep commitment for music-making that informed a large part of their identity, cultural and social life. Surely the purpose of any music education policy or practice should aspire to seek to create such rich 'musical worlds'?

Future research

The use of the CoP framework, as described by Lave and Wenger (1991, 1998, 2006, 2012), served as a useful lens for the research and was particularly instrumental in the cross-case comparison (Chapter 6). The lens provided important insights into the development of practices within a sociocultural process of learning and more specifically music-making. However, the explanatory power of the framework proved at times limiting, where the triumvirate of mutual engagement, joint enterprise and shared repertoire was somewhat confining to analyse the complex practices within CoMPs. Thus, a theoretical inter-disciplinary framework that drew upon writings of Bourdieu, Becker and de Certeau (see Chapter 1) alongside CoP concepts was employed to analyse each case separately (Chapters 3, 4 and 5). This allowed for a more nuanced and in-depth analysis to occur before applying the CoP framework to the cross-case comparison. In other words, rather than imposing categories onto the CoMPs, the practices were first analysed and then interpreted using the CoP framework. Future research should be mindful of such limitations and seek ways to combine theoretical concepts that expand existing frameworks. Broadening the theoretical scope in this study did not abandon a CoP focus but rather it served as a point of departure to extend and deepen insights into the sociocultural process of learning as it existed within musical communities.

The sample of cases caused many dilemmas within the research. Questions pertaining to how many to include, and what genres, age groups, geographical locations and settings, were all-pervasive. In seeking an in-depth understanding of three cases, across three genres, in one geographical area, in one country, representing on and offline environments, youth and adult learners, and differing stages of establishment, inevitably other potentially rich sites for investigation were omitted. Therefore, research on further geographical contexts, genres, age groups and varying stages of CoMP development would be useful to inform this relatively new area of music education and community music research. Furthermore, this research sought out existing CoMPs which predominantly rested within community settings. Thus, future research would benefit from an investigation of CoMPs within formal educational institutions. Particular questions relating to how CoMPs form and develop within a culture of teacher-learner transmission would be interesting here.

The research process relied on qualitative data only due to its appropriateness to the research questions. Methodologically the study demonstrates the powerful combination of multiple qualitative research methods to capture the group and individual 'voices' of 'musical worlds'. Through video recording, observations, interviews, participant logs and online forums, these methods increased the depth and breadth of data collection and provided for a rich analysis. It is hoped these methods and analytical approaches will inform future research approaches. Perhaps a combination of both qualitative and quantitative methods in future research may prove beneficial in broadening the contexts for understanding CoMPs.

Final thoughts

Through investigating the way CoMPs developed practices and potential for transformation in people's lives, the book presents an important 'window' into the connection between community and music. Pitts calls for (2012, p. 196) 'a need for a new emphasis on lifelong engagement as a valid aim for music education, and for a research agenda that recognises the diversity of musical lives within contemporary culture'. Strong evidence is provided across the multiple cases and rooted in everyday musical experiences about important sociocultural perspectives on musical learning, collaboration and participation within communities (both on and offline). In this way, the research challenges assumptions in varying music and education discourses about how and where such musical learning takes place. In particular, the research has stressed the importance of knowledge-building and meaning-making through music as a collaborative, 'situated' endeavour. Within this constructionist paradigm, then, the CoP model provides parameters of a theoretical framework to shape our understandings of music-making within particular sociocultural contexts.

Threats to the place and value of music and the arts appear to consistently require the need to justify funding through research. The recommendations provided for fostering sustainable CoMPs propose to bolster support for such communities into the future. The sample of cases examined represents an important contribution of practice to research. Through capturing the essence of these three musical communities, this research is informed by actual music-making practices and hopes to ultimately feed into research-led policy and practice as well as future research in this field. Thus, through participation in this study the CoMP members themselves have directly contributed to knowledge.

Turino claims (2008, p. 231), 'If we understand ourselves and our social formations in relation to habits and grasp how discourses function to construct our realities, then we gain a new freedom to shape our habits and visions of the world'. This book highlights the important place CoMPs hold within society but also within people's lives. The book intends to inform music-makers, policymakers, teachers, students, researchers and academics of the social, 'lived' collaborative learning and meaning-making that manifests itself through CoMPs. Broader music education contexts, including formal institutions, would benefit from adopting and fostering the salient characteristics of CoMPs where there is an emphasis on collective knowledge, belonging and forming of identities through community and musical practices. A CoMP approach to music education can only serve to encourage meaningful life-long musical engagement. We need to expand our view of music education to take account of these multiple and overlapping CoMPs that occur in local communities, cyberspace and across society, and seek ways to champion their development into the future. Imagine the 'wonderland' of possibilities.

Appendix A: Breakdown of data gathered

Limerick Jazz Workshop (LJW):

– 10 two-hour rehearsals (video observations)
– Two performances/gigs
– One focus group interview with participants
– Six (approx.*) individual participant logs over nine months (four entries)
– One interview with leader/organiser
– One interview with tutor

County Limerick Youth Choir (CLYC):

– 10 two-hour rehearsals (video observations)
– Two performances/gigs
– One focus group interview with participants
– 18 (approx.) individual participant logs over nine months (four entries)
– One interview with leader/conductor

Online Academy of Irish Music (OAIM):

– Eight (approx.) individual participant logs over nine months (four entries)
– OAIM discussion forums
– OAIM Facebook posts
– Two interviews with tutors
– One interview with leader/tutor

* The logs were voluntary and so while some members completed all logs, others were not as consistent. Therefore an average number was given in each case to approximate how many full logs were collected in total.

Appendix B: Interview schedules

Schedule for LJW and CLYC focus groups

1   Likes/dislikes of the CoMP

Do you like making music in this group? Why/Why not?
What do you like most about it?
Is there anything you don't like about it?

2   Actions, roles, behaviours and relationships

How would you describe your role in the group?
Do you like working with a group? What do you like/not like about it?
Do you think the group works well together? Why?
Is there any leader in this group?
How would you describe the relationships in the group?
What do you like to do most in the group?

3   Music learning and meaning making (musical/social/personal/educational)

Did you learn anything new in this group?
What did you learn about music?
Did working in a group help you to learn? How?
When you are working in the group together how does it feel?

4   Relationship between governmental support, community and music

What do you think of the support government gives through . . .?
How does this affect your group?
Is there a policy in your group that you follow?
What do you think your group's role is in the wider community?

5   Best practice and evaluation

Do your group ever review/evaluate what you are doing? How?
If not, do you think there is a need to do this? Why/Why not?
If you were in government and funding music groups like this one, what would you like to see?
What would be the best way to evaluate this do you think?

Schedule for CoMP tutors and organisers

1 Motives and expectations

What were the motives behind setting up/teaching in the XX?
What were your initial expectations?
What specifically did you want to achieve for the participants involved?
Do you think this has been achieved? How/Why not?

2 Organisation/management

How did the organisation of the XX emerge? Has this changed over time?
How would you describe your role in this group?
Has this role changed in any way over time?

3 Relationships

Do you think the group works well together? Why?
How would you describe the relationships in the group?
In what way do you think the group learns from each other?

4 Influence of government policy (international, national, local) upon communities of musical practice

Is there an overall policy or mission that your group follow?
What effect do you think government support has upon your music group?
How has this changed/not changed?
How important do you think it is for sustaining the project?
What further supports would you like to see in the future?

5 Partnership

Who are the main partners to your project?
How would you describe the relationship(s) with these partners?
What are the advantages and disadvantages of this involvement?

6 Music practice

What type of musical skills or understandings do you feel are developed from the group for the participants?
How would you describe the type of musical learning that happens?
How important is performance for the group? Why?

7 Best practice and evaluation

Do your group ever review/evaluate what you are doing? How?

8 Affordances/barriers

What do you think is the most important factor for the success of this project?
What do you feel are the main barriers to the group and how might these be rectified in the future?

Appendix C: Guiding questions for participant logs

(Sample from the Limerick Jazz Workshop (LJW))

Participant log 1

1   What age bracket are you in?
2   How long have you been with the LJW?
3   Why did you join the LJW? Please comment on your expectations when you first joined the LJW.
4   Describe what you feel your role is in the LJW at this point.
5   Has your role changed in any way since you first started with the group? If so, in what way?
6   Looking back over the past month, describe a time when you really enjoyed being a part of the LJW and why.
7   Looking back over the past month, describe a time when you did not enjoy being a part of the LJW and why.

(Qs 6 and 7 were placed at the end of all logs)

Participant log 2

1   Are you engaged in other musical activities aside from the LJW?
2   If yes, what type(s) of other musical activity are you engaged in? Please list.
3   How much time approximately do you spend each week on musical activities (this includes performing, composing, listening to music etc.)?
4   How often do you practise material for the LJW outside of the meeting time each week?
5   Describe your practising habits for the LJW (e.g. where you practise, what is your routine etc.)
6   What influence does meeting with your ensemble in the LJW have upon the way you play/sing when practising?

Participant log 3

1 How important are performance opportunities for you with the LJW?
2 Why do you think this?
3 Describe how playing/singing with the LJW at a performance feels.
4 How does playing/singing at a LJW performance differ from a LJW rehearsal?

Participant log 4

1 Describe your tutor's leadership style.
2 Are there other leaders within the group? If so, what makes them leaders?
3 Do you think you get to be creative in the LJW? If yes, explain.
4 How important is the government support that the LJW and society receive?
5 Describe what you feel are the supports given to the LJW.

Appendix D: Main findings and conclusions

(as referred to in Figure 7.1)

Figure 7.1	*FINDINGS*			*CONCLUSIONS*
CONTEXT	**Social** – interculturalism – community-building	**Cultural** – Irish/local identity	**Economic** – funding impact	CoMP practices were located and shaped within the broader macro contextual frameworks.
PRACTICES	**Musical** – formal and informal – genre-specific – collective music-making – challenge	**Community** – relationships – collaborative input – shared experiences – goal-orientated – leadership/group responsibility	**Distinctive** – creativity (LJW) – belonging (CLYC) – tradition (OAIM)	Practices emerged within a sociocultural theory of learning through socio-musical interactions.
CoMP	**Identity** – collective and individual – music-related – 'local' – overlapping and multiple	**Belonging** – socio-musical interactions and relationships – stemmed from leadership – built up over time – close-knit	**Collective knowledge** – shared input into learning experiences – lore – 'horizontalization' – peer support – leadership/collaboration	CoMPs were characterised by identity, belonging, and collective knowledge which were mutually dependent to foster and sustain CoMPs.

References

Adler, P. A., & Adler, P. (1994). Observational techniques. In N. K. Denzin & Y. Lincoln (Eds.), *Handbook of Qualitative Research*. California: Sage.

Ahlquist, K. (Ed.) (2006). *Chorus and Community*. Urbana and Chicago: Illinois University Press.

Allsup, R. E. (2003). Mutual learning and democratic action in instrumental music education. *Journal of Research in Music Education, 51*(24), 24–37.

Allsup, R. E. (2012). The moral ends of band. *Theory Into Practice, 51*(3), 179–187.

Anderson, B. (1991). *Imagined Communities: Reflections on the Origin and Spread of Nationalism* (Rev. and extended ed.). London: Verso.

Arts Council Ireland (2008a). *Points of Alignment: The Report of the Special Committee on the Arts and Education*. Dublin: Arts Council.

Arts Council Ireland (2008b). *Raising your Voice: Towards a Policy for the Development of Choral Music in Ireland*. Dublin: Arts Council.

Barrett, M. (2003). Meme engineers: Children as producers of musical culture. *International Journal of Early Years Education, 11*(3), 195–212.

Barrett, M. (2005a). Musical communication and children's communities of practice. In D. Miell, R. MacDonald & D. J. Hargreaves (Eds.), *Musical Communication* (pp. 261–280). Oxford: Oxford University Press.

Barrett, M. (2005b). A systems view of creativity. In D. J. Elliott (Ed.), *Praxial Music Education: Reflections and Dialogues* (pp. 177–195). New York: Oxford University Press.

Barrett, M. (Ed.). (2011). *A Cultural Psychology of Music Education*. Oxford: Oxford University Press.

Barton, D., & Tusting, K. (2005). *Beyond Communities of Practice: Language, Power, and Social Context*. Cambridge: Cambridge University Press.

Becker, H. S. (1998). *Tricks of the Trade: How to Think About your Research While You're Doing it*. Chicago: University of Chicago Press.

Becker, H. S. (2008). *Art Worlds* (2nd ed.). Berkeley: University of California Press.

Beineke, V. (2013). Creative learning and communities of practice: Perspectives for music education in the school. *International Journal of Community Music, 6*(3), 281–290.

Bennett, A. (2000). *Popular Music and Youth Culture: Music, Identity, and Place*. Basingstoke: Macmillan.

Benzie, D., Mavers, D., Somekh, B., & Cisneros-Cohernour, E. J. (2005). Communities of practice. In B. Somekh & C. Lewin (Eds.), *Research Methods in the Social Sciences* (pp. 180–187). London: Sage.

Berg, B. L. (2007). *Qualitative Research Methods for the Social Sciences* (6th ed.). Boston, London: Pearson/Allyn and Bacon.

Berliner, P. F. (1994). *Thinking in Jazz: The Infinite Art of Improvisation.* Chicago: University of Chicago Press.

Bithell, C. (2014). *A Different Voice, a Different Song: Reclaiming Community through the Natural Voice and World Song.* New York: Oxford University Press.

Blacking, J. (1995). *Music Culture and Experience: Selected Papers of John Blacking.* Chicago: University of Chicago Press.

Blair, D. V. (2008). Mentoring novice teachers: Developing a community of practice. *Research Studies in Music Education, 30*(2), 97–115.

Blandford, S., & Duarte, S. (2004). Inclusion in the community: A study of community music centres in England and Portugal, focusing on the development of musical and social skills within each centre. *Westminster Studies in Education, 19*(1), 7–25.

Boersma, A., ten Dam, G., Volman, M., & Wardekker, W. (2010). 'This baby . . . It isn't alive.' Towards a community of learners for vocational orientation. *British Educational Research Journal, 36*(1), 3–25.

Bogdan, R., & Biklen, S. (2007). *Qualitative Research for Education: An Introduction to Theory and Methods* (5th ed.). Boston: Pearson.

Born, G. (2010). The social and aesthetic: For a post-bourdieuian theory of cultural producation. *Cultural Sociology, 4*(2), 1–38.

Bourdieu, P. (1977). *Outline of a Theory of Practice.* Cambridge: Cambridge University Press.

Bourdieu, P. (1984). *Distinction: A Social Critique of the Judgement of Taste.* Cambridge, MA: Harvard University Press.

Bourdieu, P. (1990). *The Logic of Practice* (3rd ed.). Stanford: Stanford Universtiy Press.

Bourdieu, P. (2002). *Language and Symbolic Power* (6th ed.). Cambridge: Polity Press.

Bourdieu, P., & Johnson, R. (1993). *The Field of Cultural Production: Essays on Art and Literature.* Cambridge: Polity Press.

Bowman, W. (2007). Who is the 'we'? Rethinking professionalism in music education. *Action, Criticism, and Theory for Music Education, 6*(4), 109–131.

Bradley, D. (2009). Oh, that magic feeling! Multicultural human subjectivity, community, and fascism's footprints. *Philosophy of Music Education Review, 17*(1), 56–74.

Bruner, J. S. (1990). *Acts of Meaning.* Cambridge, MA: Harvard University Press.

Bruner, J. S. (1996). *The Culture of Education.* Cambridge, MA: Harvard University Press.

Bryman, A., & Burgess, R. G. (Eds.). (1994). *Analyzing Qualitative Data.* London: Routledge.

Burnard, P. (2002). Investigating children's meaning making and the emergence of musical interaction in group improvisation. *British Journal of Music Education, 19*(2), 157–172.

Burnard, P. (2006). The individual and social worlds of children's musical creativity. In G. McPherson (Ed.), *The Child as Musician: A Handbook of Musical Development* (pp. 353–375). Oxford: Oxford University Press.

Burnard, P. (2009). Creativity and technology: Critical agents of change in the work and lives of music teachers. In J. Finney & P. Burnard (Eds.), *Music Education with Digital Technology* (2nd ed., pp. 196–206). London: Continuum.

Burnard, P. (2012a). Commentary: Musical creativity as practice. In G. McPherson & G. Welch (Eds.), *The Oxford Handbook of Music Education* (Vol. 2, pp. 319–336). Oxford: Oxford University Press.

Burnard, P. (2012b). *Musical Creativities in Practice.* Oxford: Oxford University Press.

Burwell, K. (2012). *Studio-Based Instrumental Learning.* Farnham: Ashgate.

Campbell, P. S., & Scott-Kassner, C. (1995). *Music in Childhood: From Preschool through the Elementary Grades.* New York: Schirmer Books.

Campbell, P. S. (2002). Early childhood musical development. In L. Bresler & C. Thompson (Eds.), *The Arts in Children's Lives* (pp. 57–71). Dordrecht, The Netherlands: Kluwer Academic.

Carroll, L. (2009). *Alice's Adventures in Wonderland and Through the Looking-Glass.* Oxford: Oxford University Press.

Coffman, D. D. (2002). Adult education. In R. Colwell & C. Richardson (Eds.), *The New Handbook of Research on Music Teaching and Learning* (pp. 199–209). New York: Oxford University Press.

Cohen, L., Manion, L., & Morrison, K. (2007). *Research Methods in Education* (6th ed.). London: Routledge.

Cohen, S. (1991). *Rock Culture in Liverpool: Popular Music in the Making.* Oxford: Oxford University Press.

Cohen, S. (1994). Identity, place and the 'Liverpool sound'. In M. Stokes (Ed.), *Ethnicity, Identity and Music: The Musical Construction of Place* (pp. 117–134). Oxford: Berg.

Cohen, S. (2007). *Decline, Renewal and the City in Popular Music Culture: Beyond the Beatles.* Aldershot: Ashgate.

Colley, B., Eidsaa, R. M., Kenny, A., & Leung, B. W. (2012). Creativity in partnership practices. In G. McPherson & G. Welch (Eds.), *The Oxford Handbook of Music Education* (Vol. 2, pp. 408–426). Oxford: Oxford University Press.

Cottrell, S. (2004). *Professional Music-Making in London: Ethnography and Experience.* Farnham: Ashgate.

Countryman, J. (2009). High school music programmes as potential sites for communities of practice – a canadian study. *Music Education Research, 11*(1), 93–109.

Creswell, J. W. (2007a). *Educational Research: Planning, Conducting, and Evaluating Quantitative and Qualitative Research* (3rd ed.). Harlow: Prentice Hall.

Creswell, J. W. (2007b). *Qualitative Inquiry & Research Design: Choosing among Five Approaches* (2nd ed.). London: Sage.

Creswell, J. W. (2009). *Research Design: Qualitative, Quantitative, and Mixed Methods Approaches* (3rd ed.). Los Angeles: Sage.

Csikszentmihalyi, M. (1996). *Creativity: Flow and the Psychology of Discovery and Invention.* New York: HarperCollins Publishers, Inc.

Custodero, L. (2012). The call to create: Flow experience in music learning and teaching. In D. Hargreaves, D. Miell, & R. MacDonald (Eds.), *Musical Imaginations: Multidisciplinary Perspectives on Creativity, Performance, and Perception* (pp. 369–384). Oxford: Oxford University Press.

Davidson, J. W. & Good, J. M. M. (2002). Social and musical co-ordination between members of a string quartet: An exploratory study. *Psychology of Music, 30*(2), 186–201.

Davies, B. (2005). Communities of practice: Legitimacy not choice. *Journal of Sociolinguistics, 9*(4), 557–581.

de Certeau, M. (1984). *The Practice of Everyday Life* (S. Rendall, Trans.). Berkeley and Los Angeles: University of California Press.

DeNora, T. (2000). *Music in Everyday Life.* Cambridge: Cambridge University Press.

DeNora, T. (2003). *After Adorno: Rethinking Music Sociology.* Cambridge: Cambridge University Press.

Denscombe, M. (1999). *The Good Research Guide.* Buckingham: Open University Press.

Denzin, N. K., & Lincoln, Y. S. (2000). *Handbook of Qualitative Research* (2nd ed.). Thousand Oaks, California, London: Sage.

Department of Education and Skills & Department of Arts Heritage and the Gaeltacht (2013). *Arts in Education Charter.* Dublin: The Stationery Office.

Dillon, S. (2006). Assessing the positive influence of music activities in community development programs. *Music Education Research, 8*(2), 267–280.

Duffy, M. (2000). Lines of drift: Festival participation and performing a sense of place. *Popular Music, 19*(1), 51–64.

Durrant, C., & Welch, G. (1995). *Making Sense of Music: Foundations for Music Education.* London: Cassell.

Elliott, D. J. (1995). *Music Matters: A New Philosophy of Music Education.* New York, Oxford: Oxford University Press.

Elliott, D. J. (2005). *Praxial Music Education: Reflections and Dialogues.* Oxford: Oxford University Press.

Elliott, D. J. (2007). 'Socializing' music education. *Action, Criticism, and Theory for Music Education, 6*(4), 60–95.

Elliott, D. J., & Silverman, M. (2014). *Music Matters: A Philosophy of Music Education* (2nd ed.). New York: Oxford University Press.

Erickson, F. (2006). Definition and analysis of data from videotape: Some research procedures and their rationales. In J. L. Green, G. Camilli, & P. B. Elmore (Eds.), *The Handbook of Complementary Methods in Education Research* (pp. 177–191). Mahwah, New Jersey: Lawrence Erlbaum for American Educational Research Association.

Ewing, T. (2008). Participation cycles and emergent cultures in an online community. *International Journal of Market Research, 50*(5), 575–590.

Finnegan, R. (2007). *The Hidden Musicians: Music-Making in an English Town* (2nd ed.). Middletown, CT: Wesleyan University Press.

Finney, J., & Philpott, C. (2010). Informal learning and meta-pedagogy in initial teacher education in England. *British Journal of Music Education, 27*(1), 7–19.

Firth, S. (1993). Popular music and the local state. In T. Bennett, S. Firth, L. Grossberg, J. Shepherd, & G. Turner (Eds.), *Rock and Popular Music: Politics, Policies, Institutions* (pp. 14–24). London: Routledge.

Flynn, P. (2012). Philanthropy and Irish music education: Performance music education in Ireland. *Sonus, 33*(1), 1–10.

Folkestad, G. (2002). National identity and music. In R. MacDonald, D. J. Hargreaves, & D. Miell (Eds.), *Musical Identities* (pp. 151–162). Oxford: Oxford University Press.

Folkestad, G. (2006). Formal and informal learning situations or practices vs formal and informal ways of learning. *British Journal of Music Education, 23*(2), 135–145.

Froehlich, H. (2009). Music education and community: Reflections on 'webs of interaction' in school music. *Action, Criticism, and Theory for Music Education, 8*(1), 85–107.

Froehlich, H. (2015). *A Social Theory for Music Education: Symbolic Interactionism in Music Learning and Teaching.* New York: The Edwin Mellen Press.

Fuller, A., Hodkinson, H., Hodkinson, P., & Unwin, L. (2005). Learning as peripheral participation in communities of practice: A reassessment of key concepts in workplace learning. *British Educational Research Journal, 31*, 49–68.

Gaunt, H., & Dobson, M. C. (2014). Orchestras as 'ensembles of possibility': Understanding the experience of orchestral musicians through the lens of communities of practice. *Mind, Culture, and Activity, 21*, 298–317.

Gray, C., & Malins, J. (2004). *Visualizing Research: A Guide to the Research Process in Art and Design.* Farnham: Ashgate.

Green, L. (2002). *How Popular Musicians Learn.* Farnham: Ashgate.

Greene, M. (1982). Education and disarmament. *Teachers College Record, 84*(1), 128–136.

Greene, M. (1995). *Releasing the Imagination: Essays on Education, the Arts and Social Change.* San Fransisco: Jossey-Bass.

Greene, M. (2001). *Variations on a Blue Guitar: The Lincoln Center Institute Lectures on Aesthetic Education*. New York: Teachers College Press.

Hargreaves, D. J., Miell, D., & MacDonald, R. (2002). What are musical identities, and why are they important? In R. MacDonald, D. J. Hargreaves, & D. Miell (Eds.), *Musical Identities* (pp. 1–20). Oxford: Oxford University Press.

Harwood, E. (1998). Music learning in context: A playground tale. *Research Studies in Music Education, 11*, 52–60.

Heneghan, F. (2001). *MEND Report: A Review of Music Education in Ireland, Incorporating the Final Report of the Music Education National Debate (MEND – phase iii)*. Dublin: Dublin Institute of Technology.

Herron, D. (1985). *Deaf Ears? A Report on the Provision of Music Education in Irish Schools*. Dublin: Arts Council Ireland.

Hickey, M. (2002). The use of consensual assessment in the evaluation of children's music compositions. In C. Woods, G. Luck, R. Brochard, F. Seddon, & J. Sloboda (Eds.), *Proceedings from the Sixth International Conference on Music Perception and Cognition*. Keele: Keele University.

Higgins, L. (2007). Acts of hospitality: The community in community music. *Music Education Research, 9*(2), 281–292.

Higgins, L. (2012). *Community Music: In Theory and in Practice*. Oxford: Oxford University Press.

Holmes, J., & Meyerhoff, M. (1999). The community of practice: Theories and methodologies in the new language and gender research. *Language in Society, 28*(2), 173–183.

Humphreys, J. T. (2006). Toward a reconstruction of 'creativity' in music education. *British Journal of Music Education, 23*(3), 351–361.

John Steiner, V. (2000). *Creative Collaboration*. Oxford: Oxford University Press.

Juuti, S., & Littleton, K. (2010). Musical identities in transition: Solo-piano students' accounts of entering the academy. *Psychology of Music, 38*(4), 481–497.

Karlsen, S. (2010). Boomtown music education and the need for authenticity – informal learning put into practice in Swedish post-compulsory music education. *British Journal of Music Education, 27*(1), 35–46.

Kenny, A. (2009). *Knowing the Score: Local Authorities and Music*. Dublin: St. Patricks College, Wexford Co. Council, Sligo County Council.

Kenny, A. (2011). Mapping the context: Insights and issues from local government development of music communities. *British Journal of Music Education, 28*(2), 213–226.

Kenny, A. (2013a). Between the jigs and the reels (in cyberspace): Investigating an Irish traditional music online community. In M. Waligórska (Ed.), *Music, Longing and Belonging: Articulations of the Self and the Other in the Musical Realm* (pp. 94–113). Cambridge: Cambridge Scholars Publishing.

Kenny, A. (2013b). 'The next level': Investigating teaching and learning within an Irish traditional music online community. *Research Studies in Music Education, 35*(2), 234–248.

Kenny, A. (2013c). Sound connections for institutional practice: Cultivating 'collaborative creativity' through group composition. In P. Burnard (Ed.), *Developing Creativities in Higher Music Education: International Perspectives and Practices* (pp. 469–493). London: Routledge.

Kenny, A. (2014a). 'Collaborative creativity' within a jazz ensemble as a musical and social practice. *Thinking Skills and Creativity* (13), 1–8.

Kenny, A. (2014b). Practice through partnership: Examining the theoretical framework and development of a 'community of musical practice'. *International Journal of Music Education 32*(4), 396–408.

Kenny, A. (2016). 'Placing' technology within music education communities. In A. Ruthmann & R. Mantie (Eds.), *The Oxford Handbook of Technology and Music Education*. New York: Oxford University Press.

Kibby, M. D. (2000). Home on the page: A virtual place of music community. *Popular Music, 19*(1), 91–100.

King, N. (1994). The qualitative research interview. In C. Cassell & G. Symon (Eds.), *Qualitative Methods in Organizational Research*. London: Sage.

Koopman, C. (2007). Community music as music education: On the educational potential of community music. *International Journal of Music Education, 25*(2), 151–163.

Lamont, A. (2002). Musical identities and the school environment. In R. MacDonald, D. Miell, & D. J. Hargreaves (Eds.), *Musical Identities* (pp. 41–59). Oxford: Oxford University Press.

Lamont, A. (2011). The beat goes on: Music education, identity and lifelong learning. *Music Education Research, 13*(4), 369–388.

Lamont, A., Hargreaves, D., Marshall, N., & Tarrant, M. (2003). Young people's music in and out of school. *British Journal of Music Education, 20*(3), 229–241.

Lave, J., & Wenger, E. (1991). *Situated Learning: Legitimate Peripheral Participation*. Cambridge: Cambridge University Press.

Laycock, J. (Ed.). (2008). *Enabling the Creators: Arts and Cultural Management and the Challenge of Social Inclusion*. Oxford: European Arts Management Project in association with Oxford Brookes University.

Lenhart, A., Purcell, K., Smith, A., & Zickuhr, K. (2010). *Social Media and Mobile Internet Use among Teens and Young Adults*. Washington D.C.: Pew Internet and American Life Project.

Lincoln, Y., & Guba, E. (1985). *Naturalistic Inquiry*. London: Sage.

Littleton, K., & Mercer, N. (2012). Communication, collaboration, and creativity: How musicians negotiate a collective 'sound'. In D. J. Hargreaves, D. Miell, & R. MacDonald (Eds.), *Musical Imaginations: Multidisciplinary Perspectives on Creatvity, Performance and Perception* (pp. 233–241). Oxford: Oxford University Press.

MacDonald, R., & Wilson, G. (2005). Musical identities of professional jazz musicians: A focus group investigation. *Psychology of Music 33*(4), 395–417.

MacDonald, R., Miell, D., & Hargreaves, D. J. (2002). *Musical Identities*. Oxford: Oxford University Press.

Mans, M. (2009). *Living in Worlds of Music: A View of Education and Values*. Dordrecht: Springer.

Marsh, K. (1995). Children's singing games: Composition in the playground? *Research Studies in Music Education, 4*, 2–11.

McCafferty, D., & O'Keeffe, B. (2009). *Facing the Challenge of Change: A Spatial Perspective on Limerick*. Limerick: Limerick City Council.

McCarthy, M. (1999). *Passing it on: The Transmission of Music in Irish Culture*. Cork: Cork University Press.

Mercer, N., & Littleton, K. (2007). *Dialogue and the Development of Children's Thinking: A Sociocultural Approach*. London: Routledge.

Merriam, A. P. (1964). *The Anthropology of Music*. Evanston: Northwestern Universty Press.

Merriam, S. B. (2009). *Qualitative Research: A Guide to Design and Implementation*. San Francisco: Jossey-Bass.

Miell, D., & Littleton, K. (Eds.). (2004). *Collaborative Creativity: Contemporary Perspectives*. London: Free Association Books.

Miell, D., & Littleton, K. (2008). Musical collaboration outside school: Processes of negotiation in band rehearsals. *International Journal of Educational Research, 47*(1), 41–49.

Mok, O. N. A. (2011). Non-formal learning: Clarification of the concept and its application in music learning. *Australian Journal of Music Education* (1), 1–15.

Molloy, R., & Flynn, P. (2013). From the ground up: Creating a national infrastructure for performance music education in Ireland. In M. Schwartz (Ed.), *Foundations for Excellence 2013 Conference Proceedings* (pp. 46–54). Exeter: South West Music School.

Moore, G. (2014). Mind the gap: Privileging epistemic access to knowledge in the transition from leaving certificate music to higher education. *Irish Educational Studies, 33*(3), 249–268.

Moran, S., & John-Steiner, V. (2003). Creativity in the making: Vygotsky's contemporary contribution to the dialectic of development and creativity. In K. Sawyer, V. John-Steiner, S. Moran, R. J. Sternberg, D. H. Feldman, & J. Nakamura (Eds.), *Creativity and Development* (pp. 61–90). Oxford: Oxford University Press.

Moran, S., & John-Steiner, V. (2004). How collaboration in creative work impacts identity and motivation. In D. Miell & K. Littleton (Eds.), *Collaborative Creativity: Contemporary Perspectives* (pp. 11–25). London: Free Association Books.

Murphy McCaleb, J. (2014). *Embodied Knowledge in Ensemble Performance.* Farnham: Ashgate.

Music Network (1997). *The Boydell Papers – Essays on Music and Music Policy in Ireland.* Dublin: Music Network.

Music Network (2003). *A National System of Local Music Education Services: Report of a Feasibility Study.* Dublin: Music Network.

Ochse, R. (1990). *Before the Gates of Excellence. The Determinants of Creative Genius.* Cambridge: Cambridge University Press.

O'Flynn, J. (2009). *The Irishness of Irish Music.* Farnham: Ashgate.

Parker, E. C. (2010). Exploring student experiences of belonging within an urban high school choral ensemble: An action research study. *Music Education Research, 12*(4), 339–352.

Parker, E. C. (2014). The process of social identity development in adolescent high school choral singers: A grounded theory. *Journal of Research in Music Education, 62*(1), 18–32.

Partti, H., & Karlsen, S. (2010). Reconceptualising musical learning: New media, identity and community in music education. *Music Education Research, 12*(4), 369–382.

Pellegrino, K. (2010). *The Meanings and Values of Music-Making in the Lives of String Teachers: Exploring the Intersections of Music-Making and Teaching.* University of Michigan, Unpublished Dissertation.

Pitts, S. E. (2005). *Valuing Musical Participation.* Aldershot: Ashgate.

Pitts, S. E. (2008). Extra-curricular music in UK schools: Investigating the aims, experiences and impact of adolescent musical participation. *International Journal of Education & the Arts, 9*(10). Retrieved from http://www.ijea.org/v9n10/.

Pitts, S. E. (2009). Roots and routes in adult musical participation: Investigating the impact of home and school on lifelong musical interest and involvement. *British Journal of Music Education, 26*(3), 241–256.

Pitts, S. E. (2012). *Chances and Choices: Exploring the Impact of Music Education.* Oxford: Oxford University Press.

Plant, R. (2004). Online communities. *Technology in Society, 26*, 51–65.

Power, A. (2010). Learning through participatory singing performance. *UNESCO Observatory, 2*(1).

Prior, N. (2011). Critique and renewal in the sociology of music: Bourdieu and beyond. *Cultural Sociology 5*(1), 121–138.

Rahn, J. (2007). Digital content: Video as research. In J. G. Knowles & A. L. Cole (Eds.), *Handbook of the Arts in Qualitative Research: Perspectives, Methodologies, Examples and Issues* (pp. 299–312). London: Sage.

Robson, C. (2002). *Real World Research: A Resource for Social Scientists and Practitioner-Researchers* (2nd ed.). Malden, Massachusetts, Oxford: Blackwell Publishers.

Rubin, H., & Rubin, I. (1995). *Qualitative Interviewing: The Art of Hearing Data.* Thousand Oaks, California: Sage.

Ruthmann, S. A., & Hebert, D. G. (2012). Music learning and new media in virtual and online environments. In G. McPherson & G. Welch (Eds.), *Oxford Handbook of Music Education* (Vol. 2, pp. 567–583). Oxford: Oxford University Press.

Salavuo, M. (2006). Open and informal online communities as forums of collaborative musical activities and learning. *British Journal of Music Education, 23*(3), 253–271.

Sawyer, R. K. (2003). *Group Creativity: Music, Theater, Collaboration.* Mahwah, New Jersey: Lawrence Erlbaum Associates.

Sawyer, R. K. (2006a). Group creativity: Musical performance and collaboration. *Psychology of Music, 34*(2), 148–165.

Sawyer, R. K. (2006b). *Explaining Creativity: The Science of Human Innovation.* Oxford: Oxford University Press.

Sawyer, R. K. (2006c). Group creativity: Musical performance and collaboration. *Psychology of Music, 34*(2), 148–165.

Scahill, A. (2009). Riverdance: Representing Irish traditional music. *New Hibernia Review, 13*(2), 70–76.

Scardamalia, M., & Bereiter, C. (1991). Higher levels of agency for children in knowledge building: A challenge for the design of new knowledge media. *The Journal of the Learning Sciences, 1*(1), 37–68.

Scardamalia, M., & Bereiter, C. (1996). Student communities for the advancement of knowledge. *Communications of the ACM, 39*(4), 36–37.

Seddon, F. A., & Biasutti, M. (2009). A comparison of modes of communication between members of a string quartet and a jazz sextet. *Psychology of Music, 37*(4), 395–415.

Seddon, F. A. (2005). Modes of communication during jazz improvisation. *British Journal of Music Education, 22*(1), 47–61.

Shuker, R. (2008). *Understanding Popular Music Culture* (3rd ed.). London: Routledge.

Slobin, M. (1993). *Subcultural Sounds: Micromusics of the West.* Middletown, CT: Wesleyan University Press.

Small, C. (1998). *Musicking: The Meanings of Performing and Listening.* Middletown, CT: Wesleyan Universty Press.

Stake, R. E. (2000). Case studies. In N. K. Denzin & Y. S. Lincoln (Eds.), *Handbook of Qualitative Research* (2nd ed., pp. 435–454). Thousand Oaks, CA: Sage.

Sternberg, R. J., & Lubart, T. I. (1995). *Defying the Crowd: Cultivating Creativity in a Culture of Conformity.* New York, London: Free Press.

Sternberg, R. J., & Lubart, T. I. (1999). *The Concept of Creativity: Prospects and Paradigms.* Cambridge: Cambridge University Press.

Stewart, D. W., & Shamdasani, P. N. (1990). *Focus Groups: Theory and Practice.* Newbury Park, London, New Delhi: Sage.

Strauss, A., & Corbin, J. (1998). *Basics of Qualitative Research Techniques and Procedures for Developing Grounded Theory* (2nd ed.). London: Sage.

Turino, T. (2008). *Music as Social Life: The Politics of Participation.* Chicago: University of Chicago Press.

Tusa, J. (2007). *Engaged with the Arts: Writing from the Frontline.* London: I.B. Tauris & Co Ltd.

UNESCO (2000). *World Culture Report.* New York/Paris: UNESCO.

UNESCO (2010). *The Seoul Agenda: Goals for the Development of Arts Education.* New York/Paris: UNESCO.

UNESCO (2013). *United Nations Creative Economy Report 2013 Special Edition.* New York/Paris: UNESCO.

Veblen, K. K. (2004). The many ways of community music. *International Journal of Community Music, 1*(1), 1–15.

Veblen, K. K. (2012). Adult music learning in formal, nonformal, and informal contexts. In G. McPherson & G. Welch (Eds.), *The Oxford Handbook of Music Education* (Vol. 2, pp. 243–256). New York: Oxford University Press.

Veblen, K. K., & Olsson, B. (2002). Community music: Towards an international perspective. In R. Colwell & C. Richardson (Eds.), *The New Handbook of Research on Music Teaching and Learning* (pp. 730–753). New York: Oxford University Press.

Veblen, K. K., Messenger, S. J., Silverman, M., & Elliott, D. J. (2013). *Community Music Today.* Lanham, MD: Rowman and Littlefield Education.

Vygotsky, L. S. (1962). *Thought and Language.* New York: MIT Press/Wiley.

Vygotsky, L. S., & Cole, M. E. (1978). *Mind in Society: The Development of Higher Psychological Processes.* Cambridge, MA: Harvard University Press.

Vygotsky, L. S., Rieber, R. W., & Carton, A. S. (1993). *The Collected Works of L. S. Vygotsky.* New York, London: Plenum.

Waldron, J. (2009). Exploring a virtual music 'community of practice': Informal music learning on the internet. *Journal of Music, Technology and Education, 2*(2–3), 97–112.

Waldron, J. (2011). Conceptual frameworks, theoretical models and the role of youtube: Investigating informal music learning and teaching in online music community. *Journal of Music, Technology and Education, 4*(2–3), 189–200.

Waldron, J. (2013). YouTube, fanvids, forums, vlogs and blogs: Informal music learning in a convergent on- and offline music community. *International Journal of Music Education, 31*(1), 91–105.

Waldron, J., & Veblen, K. (2008). The medium is the message: Cyberspace, community, and music learning in the Irish traditional music virtual community. *Journal of Music, Technology and Education, 1*(2), 99–111.

Waldron, J., & Bayley, J. (2012). Music teaching and learning in the Online Academy of Irish Music: An ethnographic and cyber ethnographic field study of music, meaning, identity and practice in community. In D. D. Coffman (Ed.), *Proceedings from the International Society for Music Education (ISME) 2012 Seminar of the Commission for Community Music Activity* (pp. 62–66). Retrieved from http://issuu.com/official_isme/.

Webster, P. R. (1990). Creativity as creative thinking. *Music Educators Journal, 76*(9), 22–28.

Webster, P. R. (2011). Key research in music technology and music teaching and learning. *Journal of Music, Technology and Education, 4*, 115–130.

Wenger, E. (1998). *Communities of Practice: Learning, Meaning, and Identity.* Cambridge: Cambridge University Press.

Wenger, E. (2006). Learning for a small planet: A research agenda. Retrieved from http://www.ewenger.com.

Wenger, E. (2015). What is a community of practice? Retrieved from http://wenger-trayner.com/resources/what-is-a-community-of-practice/.

Wenger, E., McDermott, R., & Snyder, W. (2002). *Cultivating Communities of Practice: A Guide to Managing Knowledge.* Boston, MA: Harvard Business School; London: McGraw-Hill.

Wenger, E., & Snyder, W. (2000). Communities of practice: The organisational frontier. *Harvard Business Review, 78*(1), 139–146.

Wenger, E., White, N., & Smith, J. D. (2009). *Digital Habitats: Stewarding Technology for Communities.* Portland: CPsquare.

Wolff, J. (2008). *The Aesthetics of Uncertainty.* New York: Columbia University Press.

Yin, R. K. (2006). Case study methods. In J. L. Green, G. Camilli, & P. B. Elmore (Eds.), *The Handbook of Complementary Methods in Education Research* (pp. 111–122). Mahwah, New Jersey: Lawrence Erlbaum for American Educational Research Association.

Yin, R. K. (2009). *Case Study Research: Design and Methods* (4th ed.). Thousand Oaks, CA, London: Sage.

Young, S. (2003). Time-sapce structuring in spontaneous play on educational percussion instruments among three- and four-year-olds. *British Journal of Music Education, 20,* 45–60.

Zuberi, N. (2001). *Sounds English: Transnational Popular Music.* Urbana and Chicago: University of Illinois Press.

Index